PREVENTING DEER DAMAGE

ROBERT G. JUHRE

Acres U.S.A.
Austin, TX

D1264140

PREVENTING DEER DAMAGE

Acres U.S.A.
P.O. Box 91299
Austin, Texas 78709 U.S.A.
(512) 892-4400 • fax (512) 892-4448
info@acresusa.com • www.acresusa.com

Printed in the United States of America

Publisher's Cataloging-in-Publication

Juhre, Robert G., 1929-
Preventing deer damage / Robert G. Juhre. Austin, TX, ACRES U.S.A., 2011
     viii, 112 pp., 23 cm.
     Includes Index
     ISBN 978-1-60173-024-4 (trade)

     1. Deer — control. 2. Wildlife pest control. 3. Deer — food.
     4. Garden pests. I. Juhre, Robert G., 1929- II. Title.

SB994.D4 J84 2011   635.0496965

DEDICATION

This book is dedicated to my wife, Elaine, whose love of plants led to more and greater gardens every year, thus a need for deer protection led to an increasing awareness of these beautiful animals' habits. Elaine, no more! Just finish the Japanese garden and stop and enjoy.

Caution: Much of the information in this booklet is hearsay, based on folklore, reports from both amateur and professional gardeners, as well as from my own personal experience and observations.

Very little can be scientifically validated. Some of the preventative methods work some of the time, but not consistently. Some are effective in one geographic area, but not in others. Most of the manufacturer's claims are valid, but a few seem to overstate a bit.

Please, test first, so you won't be sorry later. By trial and error you will find the right method or combination of methods to deter deer from feasting at your garden table. This booklet can only inform you of the "possible" solution. A surefire guarantee is not one of the possibles.

Contents

Know Your Deer

Many people think they know a great deal about deer. Sometimes they do, but most often what they believe is erroneous. We do agree on one fact, deer eat plants and sometimes they eat YOUR plants. Here is the funny thing about it all. They don't seem to eat your weeds, but they love your favorite ornamentals.

The more you understand the habits of your backyard visitor, the better you will be able to decide on the best method to deter their marauding browsing. Deer can be a beautiful addition to your visual pleasures, and they also can make gardening and property beautification almost impossible.

The following pages will provide the information to help you decide the best method to prevent their destruction of your land-scape, in a manner that is acceptable to your particular situation. Most often, a single solution is not the answer, but several of the

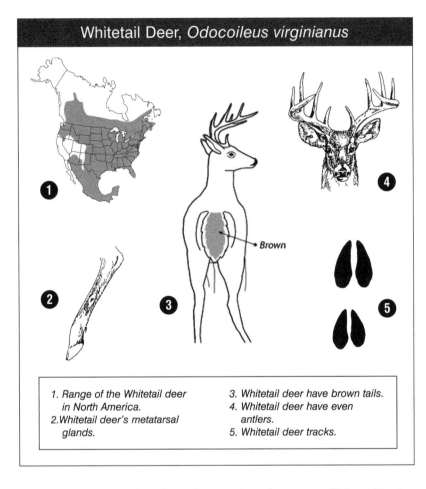

Whitetail Deer, *Odocoileus virginianus*

Brown

1. Range of the Whitetail deer in North America.
2. Whitetail deer's metatarsal glands.
3. Whitetail deer have brown tails.
4. Whitetail deer have even antlers.
5. Whitetail deer tracks.

deer deterrents outlined in the coming chapters will be effective when used in conjunction with each other. You will find some solutions work fine for a period of time, but then lose their effectiveness and must be changed. This is often true when using repellents.

The Whitetail Deer — *Odocoileus virginianus* — occurs in every state in the lower United States plus Canada and Mexico. It has been introduced successfully in many other parts of the world, including such diverse locations as Stewart Island, located south of South Island, New Zealand, and to private zoos around the world. In many areas of this country it is over-abundant and increasing in numbers each year. This prolific animal had adapted well to man's encroachment of its habitat and has actually benefited from deforestation and urbanization. The whitetail continues to survive so well partly because it has a wide range of plants it will forage on (in excess of 500). It is also elusive, cautious, somewhat nocturnal and adapts well to a wide range of environments. It is comfortably at home in rural farmlands, suburban developments, and even urban areas. This means they are in your backyard.

The reduction or elimination of the whitetails' natural predators left the annual hunting season, some poaching and the automobile as the only control factors. At times, severe winters or food shortages will slow down the growth of the herds, but that is only a temporary happening and recovery is usually rapid. In some counties, where the deer herds are particularly dense, there are known to be two kinds of drivers, those that have hit a deer with their car or truck and those that will.

In the mid 1800's, the whitetail deer was virtually eliminated in the six northeastern states and was rare in four others. By 1900, Connecticut was experiencing a comeback, with 200 deer reported in the entire state. What a far cry from today's booming population. The total deer population in the entire country was estimated at 500,000 at that time. By 1964, there were an estimated 8,000,000 deer throughout the country and by 2007, some experts estimate there were 30,000,000 deer nationally. This means a serious over-abundance of deer in some parts of the country.

The same population explosion has occurred with both the elk and antelope herds for the same reason.

| 1990 | 41,000 Elk | 1990 | 12,000 Pronghorn |
| 1995 | 800,000 Elk | 1995 | 1,000,000 Pronghorn |

Virtually every other animal has experienced serious declines due to human intrusion into their habitat or severe altering of that habitat. Not the whitetail.

To help control the overpopulation problem, some states issue doe hunting permits, others have certain zones of high density deer populations where more than one deer may be shot during a single season on one license. Some states have taken more drastic measures and "harvest" permits are issued to control the herds when normal hunting seasons have not reduced the numbers adequately. Today, Texas, Mississippi, New Jersey, Minnesota, Michigan,

Pennsylvania and New York have the largest whitetail populations. Interestingly, both sexes are increasing in numbers, not just does. It is also interesting to note that the states with the largest number of deer are in the populous East and not in the wilds of the West. The suburbanization of the East has been beneficial to the deer herds.

There are some regional differences within the species. The more dramatic being the small Florida Key deer and the equally small San Juan Island deer of Washington State. Some eight to ten subspecies have been identified, but most biologists agree that we are still dealing with the same animal — the Virginia Whitetail deer (the San Juan deer is a blacktail species).

Some writers infer that the whitetail is an Eastern deer and the mule deer or the blacktail is the Western deer. Sorry! The West has both white and blacktail deer with their territories sometimes overlapping.

Some of the subspecies mentioned by authoritative sources are the Eastern whitetail, the Virginian whitetail, the Northern Virginian deer, the Florida deer, the Key deer, Coues deer, Louisiana whitetail and the Texas whitetail. Whether these are truly subspecies or whether it's like calling a cougar, a painter, a panther, a catamount, a puma or a mountain lion, is debatable by some. At any rate, regardless of what's in a name, they're all the same animal.

The Western mule deer or the blacktail have habits similar to the whitetail when it comes to harassing gardeners. In spite of differences in range and some behavioral differences, most of the methods of deterring deer will apply to both.

If you are a Westerner, you know that a "muley" can readily be identified by its pronging gait when startled, its large mule like ears, black tail and its antler arrangement. Practiced hunters will also note the subtle differences in their tracks.

The most common misconception regarding the whitetail is relative to its size. Almost everyone, even the experienced hunters and outdoors persons, will overestimate its height. When asked how tall a deer is at its shoulders, most observers will put their hand at shoulder height when indicating a deer's height. Wrong! Belt level would be closer to its actual height. The average whitetail is only 36" to 40" high at the shoulder.

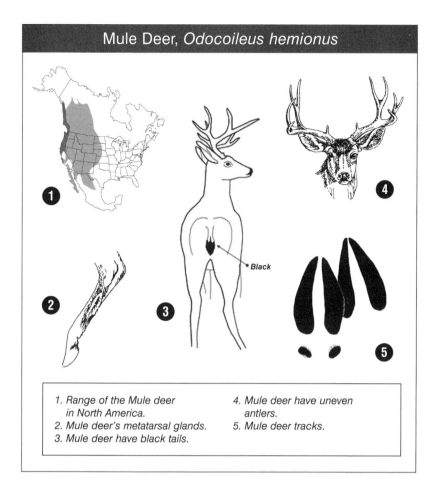

Mule Deer, *Odocoileus hemionus*

1. Range of the Mule deer in North America.
2. Mule deer's metatarsal glands.
3. Mule deer have black tails.
4. Mule deer have uneven antlers.
5. Mule deer tracks.

Most people also overestimate their length, which is 5' to 6' long. When it comes to weight, the inexperienced (and sometimes the experienced) are generally way off — on high side. The average deer weighs in at about 150 pounds live weight. It probably seems like 250 pounds if you just hauled it out of a gully or through heavy brush for a mile or so.

The Florida Key deer will weigh in at no more than 75 to 80 pounds and the largest whitetail on record is 425 pounds. Much heavier deer have been reported, but not authenticated.

The deer's coloration will vary from area to area and they will differ from season to season. All deer shed their hair twice a year. Once in the spring when they attain a reddish brown color and again in the fall when their winter coat appears as a duller gray or even a bluish brown.

Although there are some regional differences and even some unusual mutations, most whitetails look essentially the same. There is a subspecies on the San Juan Islands in the State of Washington that have a pinto coloration and are about the same size as the Florida Key deer or perhaps even a little smaller. There is also a deer herd on a large military installation in New York State that have a light gray color and almost appear white. They are not albinos. Albinism is not unknown among deer, but the lack of coloration usually leads to an early demise.

Only the males (bucks) have horns, other than rare aberrations where a doe will sport a pair of horns. A whitetail's antlers have all their points growing off the main stems, unlike a mule deer. The size of the antlers will vary in different parts of the country and even in parts of a geographical range. Biologists believe this is due to the mineral content of the forage as well as genetic disposition. Very often you will find large trophy bucks in farm country where the living is easy and the food is plentiful. On the other hand, it is true that the Texas brush country consistently produces large trophy heads.

Certain micro-ecosystems in other parts of the country are also known for their large deer. Genetics, healthy eating or a combination therof probably contributes to the size of the rack.

Both sexes have black noses with two white bands beside it. A brown face with brown eyes encircled in white is typical. The inside of the ears, under the chin, and the large throat patch are white. As the name implies, the underside of the tail and the inside part of the rear legs are also white. The top of the tail is brown with a black stripe running down the center.

When alarmed, whitetails erect their tails and flare their rump hairs as alarm signals. This behavior is more common with does than with bucks. This flashing white signal can readily be seen by other deer, even at night or in the dark reaches of the forest. Hence, the whitetail. Under extreme stress, when deer prefer not to flag, they may make a series of barking sounds.

The feeding habits of the whitetail depend upon the availability of food, size of the herd, limitations of the range, and weather conditions. When an abundance of food is available, the deer will restrict its travel to about one square mile. Severe winter weather may force them into lower elevations and even to the relative protection of urban areas. During winter, many plants that are not bothered by deer during the other seasons now become part of their diet.

Deer will eat a wide variety of vegetation. They are browsers as opposed to grazers, although they are not opposed to munching on a good alfalfa field or your lawn if the grass is long enough. Deer feed very rapidly. Being ruminants with four compartment stomachs, they initially chew their food just enough to swallow it. This food gets stored in the area called the rumen. From there it is regurgitated, then re-chewed before being swallowed again, entering a second stomach where digestion begins. Then it is passed into the third and fourth stomachs, finally entering the intestine. Truly a remarkable system which allows deer to feed rapidly when exposed to possible dangers, and then to finish the process in the safety of a secluded place.

The more plentiful the food and the more secure the feeding area, the more slowly they feed. In your yard, it could be a nibble here, a nibble there, a nibble everywhere. If the tidbit is incredibly tasty, they may devour the entire planting. Plants grown on fertilized soil seem to appeal even more, possibly due to the salts and minerals taken up into the plant. Water scarcity also plays a major role in deer diet. During droughts, deer will browse plants like succulents they normally avoid.

Deer need about 10 to 12 pounds of food each day. At that rate, you can see what a deer can do to your landscape. Make it three or four deer and you have devastation. Deer will usually start feeding about 4:30 in the afternoon in the summertime and continue for several hours. They may feed again during the night and early morning for a like period of time. In urban areas, you may find them feeding at any time. When not feeding they are generally lying low in dense cover, preferably on a ridge, if available, where odors can waft up to them and they can command a view of the lower elevations.

Their sense of smell is acute. Deer find food with their nose, keep track of other deer in the territory with their nose, avoid danger with their nose and rely on their nose for mating purposes. Therefore, odors offensive to their nose can repel deer and keep them away from your favorite plants. Deer have hairless noses, which helps their sense of smell. Most odors are organic compounds which are released as molecules of gas. For gases to be smelled, they must be mixed with water or some other liquid.

Their hearing and sight are also keen. Deer are color blind and see in monochromic shades of gray. When they see a flag tied to a wire that is strung two feet above a ten foot fence, they perceive the fence to be twelve feet high. I think this might be called Gestalt configuration — where the individual elements cannot be separated from the whole. Their hearing is at the higher registry of sound, which is why some of the noisemaking devices described later seem to work. A deer's sense of taste is also highly developed and quite discriminate. Its preference is for plants with a tender, juicy content and a bland flavor. This fact is going to help us to find ways to prevent their deprivation. Deer have several different scent glands. Their metatarsal glands are on the outside of both legs and emit an ammonia-like smell. Interdigital glands are located between their toes and help mark the trail.

Most people have the impression that deer are extremely fast. With their senses so highly developed they don't have to be excessively fast. Their actual top speed is about 35-40 miles per hour. The hare will hit a top speed of 50 miles per hour. Many animals are faster than deer, especially for short spurts. But even at 30 miles per hour a deer can still cover a lot of territory. A deer can clear a six foot fence with little effort from a standing still position. It can also leap 25 to 30 feet when on the run. A deer can jump high! A deer can jump far! But, a deer cannot jump high and far at the same time. When a deer jumps an obstacle, it will take off just inches from the barrier. A deer prefers to go under a fence rather than expose itself by jumping over it.

When motivated, it needs only to get its head through an opening and the rest of the body probably can follow. Fawns can penetrate incredibly small openings. If a fawn finds a way into your fenced yard and becomes separated from its mother, the resulting panic is pure havoc. The behavioral attributes that you are reading about are important when you begin to decide which type of deer protection is right for you.

Many people think deer are mute because they have never heard them utter a sound. Not so. They make a wide variety of sounds. Fawns bleat like lambs. Does can sound like sheep. They also whistle, bark, snort and grunt. They communicate by stamping their feet and flashing that white tail. They use the scent glands on their legs, feet and heads to mark their passing.

A bucks' antlers reach full size in September. He will rub them against trees and bushes to remove the velvet. This can cause considerable damage to your ornamentals. Later, by November, when the buck is in rut and has raging hormones, he may polish his horns against your trees as well as doing mock battles with saplings and shrubs. This can be even more destructive than the velvet removal process. When he shadow boxes your ornamentals, he turns, thrusts, twists, pushes, pulls and parries. Damage can be devastating, with all the appearances of a war zone. Even a deer can be aggressive when in rut. A large midwestern paper reported the story of a man on his way to work in an affluent suburb, when he was chased and ultimately treed by an amorous buck defending his territory. There are also innumerable stories of incautious hunters being gored by the downed deer they had shot. This probably is a case of the deer's frantic struggle and attempt to escape, rather than an act of aggression.

A doe's gestation period is about 200 days. She can come into heat up to four times in a single season if not impregnated on earlier tries. Normally, she will be bred during her first or second heat, but occasionally during the last heat. This explains why some fawns are still spotted in late fall. They were just born late.

In areas where food is plentiful, twins are common and triplets are not rare. Quadruplets are not unheard of, although I personally have never seen a quad. As soon as a fawn is born, the doe licks it clean and bonding begins. In about ten minutes the fawn can wobble along and the doe will lead it away from the birthing area to another place of concealment. The doe will then move a hundred feet or so from where the fawn is hidden and bed down. She will return six to eight times a day to nurse her fawn. A fawn instinctively knows not to move during times of danger. They also give off no odor during these early weeks. The spotted coat provides almost perfect camouflage. Fawns are only five or six pounds in weight when born, but quickly gain weight and increase in size.

A whitetail's normal life span is eight to eleven years. Bucks reach maturity at five, but seldom live that long, except in remote areas free from hunting pressures and automobiles. Does continue to bear at least one fawn a year for most of their life span, although fertility does decrease around the ninth year.

If your property is being browsed by deer, you will see telltale signs. You will find browsed leaves and twigs, eaten buds, fruit and berries being stripped from brambles. You may find some plants pulled entirely out of the ground. A deer has no teeth in the front of its top jaw, so each bite results in a jagged impression.

You will also recognize the sharp pointed split hoof prints. Droppings are easily recognized, but may differ winter from summer. The pellets in winter are hard, brown, and about three-quarters of an inch in length, due to its winter diet of conifers and brush. In the summer, the pellets will be a lighter colored brown, softer and more tube shaped. If a buck has used one of your favorite ornamentals for an antler rub, you will see it from afar.

Deer are creatures of habit. They usually show up at the same time each day, follow the same trails, take the route of the least resistance and generally behave in a predictable manner.

Availability of food, severe weather and external interference (such as dogs or construction activity) can alter their habitual ways. But, like most things in life, they are a contradiction and will act quite unpredictably at times. There are innumerable instances of deer entering public buildings in suburban areas, often through a window, which unfortunately wasn't open. There are many stories of seemingly unpredictably bizarre behavior. Perhaps if we knew all the events and circumstances that led up to that behavior it would be more understandable? Now that you have read this far, you know more about the whitetail deer than your average, "I'm gonna get my big buck this year," hunter. Want to confirm this? Ask him or her to indicate with their hands how high the average whitetail is at the shoulder. Remember the answer? Anything over belt high just isn't so. Thirty-six to forty inches is the average height. If they miss the correct answer, you'll probably hear this excuse. "I thought you meant how tall was it to the top of its head." Sure you did.

2

Look at Your Problem, Then Figure Out the Solution

Only you can decide what kind of deer protection is most suitable for your needs. Carefully think through the following questions. They will help you decide which method or combination of methods meet your needs. Sometimes a rough drawing of your property, indicating the areas to be protected, can be helpful in analyzing the overall problems.

1. What is the size of the area to be protected?
2. Must the entire area be protected or just certain parts?
3. Are there visual constraints? Your own sense of aesthetics. Your neighbors view? Passersby's? Community regulations?
4. Is the area to be protected formal, informal or natural?

5. How labor intensive is any solution being considered? Does it require maintenance on an on-going basis?

6. Is the need for protection only temporary? Just to protect young trees for a few years.

7. Is the solution permanent or temporary? If temporary, how often will it have to be renewed?

8. Does the solution require constant maintenance? How often? How costly?

9. How expensive is the solution? Does it appear to be cost effective?

10. Are there any dangers or hazards involved with the chosen solution?

11. Is the solution neighborhood friendly? Will it meet local ordinances? Is there a homeowners' association to deal with?

12. How effective is the solution based on known facts?

13. Are there any other alternative methods, even if not as effective, that should be considered for other reasons?

14. Will the deer problem solution be satisfactory longterm?

15. Will the deer have to be totally excluded or is a compromise possible?

The following chapters will describe various solutions to deter deer from being a perennial pest. One or more will suit your needs. It is important to protect your plants and landscape, but be sensible and don't overkill. It may help you to write the questions previously listed on a piece of paper, then put the correct responses next to the questions. In this way, you may get a clearer picture of what you are trying to accomplish and the best methods to achieve the maximum results. If the problem is simple, like one favorite ornamental or a single garden area, the solutions are fairly easy to figure out. It's those complex situations of multiple garden areas, persnickety neighbors and other variables that make this quest a challenge at best and a frustration at worst.

Here's an example:

Evaluation Question	Response
1. Size of area	Small
2. Entire area or part	Entire
3. Visual constraints	Neighbors
4. Formal or informal	Patio
5. Etc.	

This little exercise may seem too elementary, but by doing so you will more readily be able to discard the ideas that aren't right for you, leaving the better choices to think about.

3
Shooting, Trapping & Removal

In most instances, the legal shooting of deer during the hunting season, if allowed in your locale, will do little to reduce the deer population on any long-term basis. Additional deer will move into your habitat to replace those removed the year before. This is not the case with heavy poaching, where fawns, pregnant does, and many of the breeding bucks are removed. Even in that severe scenario, the deer herd will be replaced with deer from adjacent areas.

The same is true, when allowed, of trapping or removal by other means. Eventually, other deer will move into the vacated space.

Thinning of herds by professional hunters has been used by some municipalities to reduce foraging in heavily populated areas or where travel becomes dangerous due to deer movement across well-traveled roads. Providing the entire herd is removed, this will only be temporarily effective. If there is adequate cover and food, eventually the deer will return. This method is generally not acceptable to animal activist groups. Unfortunately, attempting to remove the herd by using drugs often results in many deaths and a new problem arises when attempting to relocate the deer to a new area.

A well-to-do area in New York State tried darting the does with a birth control drug. This particular drug required more than one dose to be effective. The biologists now faced a simple problem. Which doe had received its first shot? The next year they tried to dart and color code each deer. Normal human-type conception control does not work on deer. The estrogen in regular birth control maintains the females' estrus and the bucks remain in rut disrupting the herd. Contraception is a better method. A vaccine called PZP has been used to control the wild horse herd on Assateague Island and the deer herd on Fire Island. It works for small populations but is probably not practical in places like Potter County, Pennsylvania with 100,000 deer.

Elimination is not a practical nor desirable solution. Protection of your individual property is a better answer. Coexistence is possible and for many, the only solution.

Game management by sterilization, tranquilizing, germ implants and cervix birth control generally have not been effective due to their costs, practicability or public opposition. All we can predict for the near future are larger and healthier deer herds.

Fences

Fences are good for defense, but do it early. If fencing is to be part of your strategy to protect a new project, do it before you plant that orchard or till that vegetable garden. Not only is it easier to build while the land is vacant, it is better that the deer do not establish a habit of visiting the area to be planted. We will cover a variety of fence choices in this section. Weigh these alternative ideas carefully. Some are relatively expensive; some require maintenance; some are unsightly; some are time intensive for the do-it-yourselfer and some are oriented for specific needs. Because these various fencing solutions vary greatly in cost, appearance and effectiveness, they may be only part of your overall plan. At this point, we are assuming you are trying to keep deer out, not coexist.

Wood Fence with Sheep Wire — 12 Foot High

A 12' high fence, constructed of treated 4" x 4"s, set on a concrete base that is below the frost line, should have a 30-year life. Remember, your entrance gate needs to be the same height. Use 2" x 4" cross bars to firm up the corners or cables with turn buckles which can be used for the same purpose. Now attach 6' sheep wire with 4" mesh to the lower section of the posts that have been set on ten foot centers. Tighten each section with a fence stretcher (usually available at rental stores) and fasten the wire to the posts with galvanized staples. After the lower section is completed, follow the same procedure for the upper run of fencing wire. Attach the lower and upper runs of sheep fencing together with pig rings. These can be found at farm stores along with a special pliers-like tool for closing them easily. If 6' high sheep wire is not available, then use 4' high wire. Now your installation is only 8' high. To reach the desired 10 feet, you will have to string two runs of wire, a foot apart, across the upper two feet of space.

If you are bothered by other small critters, this is the time to keep them out as well. Purchase some 2' high, 1" mesh chicken wire. Dig a trench 6" deep and place the wire in the bottom of the trench. Using the appropriate sized smaller galvanized staple, attach the wire to the bottom of the fence posts.

Fill in the trench with the soil you had previously removed. Now, you have an effective barrier against rabbits, gophers, grouse and other small creatures. You have not solved the raccoon or woodchuck problem at this point. That will take an entirely different approach. An electric wire, one foot high, will take care of them.

Costs of material will vary in different parts of the country. No matter where you live, this fence is expensive, labor intensive and probably visually offensive if you live in a suburban area. It also requires some specialized tools, such as either a manual or gas powered post hole digger, a wire fence stretcher, pig ring pliers, as well as the more common tools such as a hammer, saw, 4' level, shovel and a lot of heart. This fence can be installed by one person, but two make it a lot easier.

Remember that deer have a propensity to go under a fence if at all possible. If you haven't put the buried chicken wire barrier on your fence, then make sure that the bottom of the fence reaches the ground around the entire perimeter. This will not be the case, unless you build on a perfectly level place. You can fill this space with rocks, logs or string wire along the bottom of the fence.

There are advantages of this formidable super fence. It will last into the foreseeable future, it is maintenance free, it is impervious to inclement weather and climatic upheavals. It deters deer and other small creatures. I have heard reports of deer clearing a twelve foot fence, but have never authenticated such reports. Perhaps the person reporting such a feat left the gate open?

Fence Modification

This same basic fence design can be modified in many ways. I have personally found that an 8' fence (using 10' posts) is very effective. I would still use pressure treated posts (and also those that are insect resistant) if needed in your area. It is possible to purchase untreated posts and treat the part being buried with a preservative. Don't use toxic materials.

There are major cost savings in building a shorter fence. Not only are your posts less costly, but you can use 4' high sheep wire. It will also be easier to construct than the super fence. If you don't set your posts in concrete your costs go down some more and your labor decreases. You will want to go below your frost line to prevent winter heaving. If you are concerned about the height of the 8' fence, you could add a short 2" x 4" to the top of each post and run a 14-gauge wire between the risers. You now have effectively increased the height of your fence by the height of the additions. It is not as attractive, but less expensive and just as effective. The use of ribbon wire not only makes the height even more visible to deer, but also to humans.

Outriggers

Regardless of whether you use treated timbers, cedar posts or other wood products, they still have a limited life depending on the amount of moisture content in your soil. Setting your posts in concrete bases and attaching the posts to the base with a variety of metal devices will prevent a rot problem. Once again, it's expensive and time consuming. If this is your inclination, a visit to the nearest arboretum should provide you with different methods of attachment. In wet areas this may be desirable.

Another means to an end to prevent deer from jumping a shorter fence is to attach outriggers at a 90 degree angle to your posts about 18" from the bottom. Attach a wire to these outriggers, which can be made from 2" x 4"s or even 2" x 2"s. They should extend out from the posts about 24". Now, when deer approach the fence, its legs hit the wire and it is too far away from the fence for a comfortable jump. Deer like to be close to the object to be cleared. It's part of that high and far idea. An electric wire in this position is even more effective.

Uneven Ground

Just another reminder. Whatever type of barrier you construct, be sure the bottom area is secure or a deer, and particularly a fawn, will slip under the barrier. Use wire, dirt, rocks or logs to fill the space. If there is any slack in the fencing a 2" space can open up enough to allow a smaller deer under the fence.

Metal Post Fence with Sheep Wire

First, install 6' metal fence posts at 10' intervals. Then attach 4" square opening sheep wire to the posts with wire clips. Take eight foot steel posts and wire them to the top of your vertical steel posts. Place the bottom of the posts in the ground at a 45 degree angle. Now attach 14-gauge wire along the angled posts at 6" intervals.

You now have a fence virtually impenetrable by most any animal. Some people claim this type of barrier fence is adequate without the mesh sheep wire on the upright posts. The slanted outrigger posts with the wire strung on them will keep out any deer, horse or cow. The entire fence is too wide and tall for an animal to jump over and they are reluctant to step between the 6" spaced wires. Frankly, if I considered a fencing system this elaborate, I wouldn't eliminate the vertical sheep wire.

This is an expensive system, labor-intensive, as durable as steel posts are in your climate and absolutely deer proof.

Electric Fences

Electric fences have been extensively tested and recommended by many universities. They do work well in many instances, but there are certain factors that can make them ineffective or at least, not 100% deer proof. There may be legal implications.

Recommendations range from using a 6' high metal post installation with seven strands of wire to a four wire installation. The wire must be attached to the posts with insulators and also grounded with a metal post in a moist medium. The newer fiberglass posts do not require insulators. They are lightweight and can be easily moved as they are only in the ground a few inches. The poly wire is also much easier to handle than the 14-gauge wire usually used in the metal post or wooden post systems. If you live in arid areas you may have to moisten the ground where you have driven the ground post.

Ecologists from the University of Wisconsin have experimented with single strand electric fences. The wire was smeared with peanut butter at regular intervals. Peanut butter, or some other deer delicacy, is essential to lure the deer into an initial nose shock. The deer's hollow hair is not a great conductor of electricity, but its hairless nose is quite vulnerable. The test areas were 36 corn fields in prime Wisconsin deer country. The test was virtually 100% effective. However, there were unprotected adjacent corn fields the deer could feed on. Although the deer could obviously jump this low fence, it seems the initial shock was enough to keep them away. Would this work if there was no choice food nearby? That variable was not tested.

The electric fence can be powered by house current, A/C, D/C or solar powered energizer with storage batteries to provide power during the night or cloudy days. Be sure your battery chargers or energizers are weatherproof. Some are not and need to be protected. A simple tester is available to determine if your fence is either hot or off. An interrupter device breaks the current at short intervals to prevent anyone from becoming "stuck" on the hot wire. Touching the wire while standing on wet ground or grass can be especially troublesome. Do not try to determine if the fence is on by touching it with a piece of grass or green stick. If you do, you'll get zapped.

There are many advantages to the electric fence approach. It's fairly easy to install (a one person job). It's relatively inexpensive, once you have your charger. It's not too obtrusive and can cover a very large area. It has a few disadvantages. It should be identified as an electric fence to warn unsuspecting people. It should be kept clear of weeds or other debris to avoid potential shorting which could possibly cause a fire in dry country and also keep the fence from conducting properly. I have heard many reports that the fence can be turned off once the fawns have been conditioned to the shock properties of the peanut butter coated wire. I'm not totally confident with this. When constructing the "Architecturally Designed Fence" (see description later in chapter), a traditional fence is constructed for the lower 4' and a 4 strand electric fence is installed for the top 4'. Some dispute the need for electrifying the wire, as the deer would not be grounded if jumping the fence. Perhaps the bottom wire should be electric and baited with peanut butter.

Electric Deer Netting

The concept is similar to the regular deer netting fence covered later in this chapter. Each horizontal wire is electrified on the electric netting fence. This method can be suitable for a relatively small area with a large deer population.

There are many advantages to the electric mesh fence approach. If properly constructed, it not only keeps deer out, but also raccoons, woodchucks and the neighbors dogs. Although not invisible, it ranks pretty high on the visual acceptability scale. For a small area, it's not too expensive and can be easily installed by one person. The wire mesh fence has the same cautions as the standard electric fence, the shock factor to the unsuspecting, fire hazards in dry country, shorting potential and even protests from animal rights activists.

Elevated Chicken Wire Barrier

Purchase 4' wide, 2" mesh opening chicken wire. Lay this around the perimeter of the property to be protected. The wire then needs to be raised about 18" off the ground. To keep the wire at the desired height you can drive stakes into the ground every 10 to 12 feet and string wire between the posts or lay a board across the posts. It is simpler and just as effective to stretch the chicken wire taunt between the posts and staple it in place. Laying the wire over brush or limbs is equally effective, but may sag after time. This barrier fence acts like a cattle guard that you see across roads. Deer will not step through the wire and generally will not be able to jump it if it has been installed at the correct height. This can be an expensive way of protecting a cultivated area and there can be a problem if the wire becomes covered with a heavy growth of vines, such a vetch or kudzu, and loses its effect.

Double Post with Mesh Wire Fence

We know deer cannot jump high and far. Based on that principle, a very effective fence can be built to form a double barrier. If a short fence already exists, this solution can be even more viable.

First, install a 4' fence using metal or wood posts. Place them every ten to twelve feet apart and stretch 2" mesh chicken wire between the posts, if the barrier is to be temporary. Use sheep wire if a permanent installation is required. If an existing fence can be incorporated into the plan, you have just saved one half of the labor and materials required for this type fence. Now, install a second 4' fence 30" from the first fence. By leaving only 30" of space between the two fences, you prevent the deer from jumping the first fence, landing in the space between and then jumping the second fence. Again, use either chicken wire or sheep wire, depending on your needs. I have heard that three feet is high enough to accomplish this no jump barrier, but I'm little conservative and would prefer the higher fence. Alternate the placement of the second set of posts to center on the space between the first set of posts.

If you are in an area where you can obtain your own fence posts from State or Federal land at no cost, this is a particularly good approach. On the other hand, if you need to purchase the posts, they are half the size needed for a high barrier fence. This is also a labor intensive installation when you consider digging a double row of post poles, cutting and transporting the posts, peeling the posts and finally installing them.

If you have access to posts, the time and the energy — this one works. Here's the bonus. You can raise chickens or other fowl between the fences. Try guinea hens. They're pretty and noisy.

Double Fence Variation

After installing your first fence or utilizing an existing fence, install a secondary electric fence 30" from the first fence, at a height of 22" to 24" from the ground. Remember? A deer wants to be close to the barrier to be jumped. When it approaches the fence its legs will come in contact with the electric wire and receive a mild shock. The hair is not as thick on the deer's front legs and offers no insulation.

If you are concerned that the deer might slip under the fence, then install two strands of electric wire, one 6" off the ground and the top wire 24" high.

The advantages are apparent. You incur modest costs and less labor when installing the second fence using plastic posts and poly wire. The cautions are the same as with any electric fence.

Additional Modifications

If you are nervous about the effectiveness of your two fence system or if the snickering of your non-believer neighbor is beginning to bother you, you can install one or two of the following additions.

Install a post that is 6' high every third post. If this is an existing fence, nail a 2" x 4" to every third post to increase its height. Staple a wire across the top of the taller posts or the extensions that you have added to the short posts. This heightening of the fence should be made to the fence closest to the area to be protected (the inside fence). Tying plastic colored forestry markers at regular intervals will make the fence more visible and the illusion of height will be enhanced. Ribbon wire will accomplish the same thing.

Nail a two foot 2" x 2" or 2" x 4" board perpendicular to every third post. This installation should be on the outside fence (the one furthest from the area to be protected). Staple a wire onto these extensions. This could also be an electric wire if desired. You now have a powerhouse system that can be installed around relatively large areas at a fairly nominal material cost, but huge outlays of energy. Let the neighbors laugh, this fence will stop the most persistent deer.

Plastic Fencing

These barriers are sometimes called deer netting and can be used to protect individual trees, bushes or installed as a regular fence. Most are made of polypropylene and will not rust or rot. They are strong, durable, and resistant to both herbicides and UV light.

The rolls of plastic fencing are lightweight and easy to handle during installation, which is fairly simple. Mesh openings are usually 2 1/2" x 2 1/2". This is a relatively sound solution for small areas. The 7 1/2' height offers adequate protection in most areas where the deer have alternative choices for feeding. Manufacturers claim it only needs support every 30' feet and can be attached directly to growing trees. Due to its flexibility, it can be snaked around your plantings to create a more natural appearance.

Some of these barriers are difficult to see through. If a deer can't see over a barrier and can't see through it, it's reluctant to jump over it. In fact, some manufacturers supply white cloth streamers to notify the deer after the plastic barrier is installed that they have something to contend with. These streamers can be removed after the deer realize their former right of way is now blocked. The plastic netting's relative invisibility is a great asset when aesthetics are important.

The Natural Hedge Fence

A natural hedge barrier is a slick way of keeping a deer from your vulnerable areas, providing you can keep the deer from eating it while it is getting established or plant a hedge that is not palatable to the deer. Spraying the leaves in the spring with a deer repellent is desirable. You could also protect them with netting during the tender growth period.

There are many kinds of bushes that will form a fine deer barrier. You will want to choose one that does well in your climate and is fast growing, thick and full at the bottom and will attain a height of eight feet or more or a width of six feet. The following shrubs can be used effectively and there are many more available if you check with your local nurseries or county extension services. Osage orange, Caragana (Siberian peashrub), rambling hedge roses or shrub roses, barberry, privet, Siberian or Chinese elm and blackberry are all suitable for hedges. Some of these shrubs are drought resistant, others are heat tolerant, cold resistant and disease free.

Some can be sheared or pruned to keep them contained at an acceptable height or from spreading more than necessary. The problem of protecting these shrubs while waiting for them to reach maturity is a temporary situation. Most of those mentioned are not high on the deer gourmet eating list. Often your state conservation department, county extension service or other local agencies can supply seedlings suitable for your climatic conditions, usually at no or little cost.

You could install the double chicken wire fence or an electric fence to temporarily keep the deer from eating the living fences until they mature. As the hedge grows to maturity, it will completely envelope the chicken wire fence so it will no longer be seen. By not removing the wire fence, you have reinforced the living fence and made it more impenetrable.

A gardener in Minnesota reports remarkable success by planting a row of tall sunflowers along her garden's perimeter. When approaching the sunflowers, the deer stopped at about fifteen feet from them and backed off. She also laid sunflower stalks over her new strawberry bed and the deer stopped nibbling the new plants. Will it work for you? Maybe not, but it's worth a try.

Architecturally Designed Fences

In many suburban yards you are dealing with a relatively small area to contain. By using existing buildings as part of your enclosure, along with attractive gates, finished posts, arches and other designs common to well-designed property fences, you can create a most pleasing deer fence. The fence still has to be high, but at least it can be aesthetically acceptable. The cost will be high also. Most large garden centers should be able to help you with your design or you can hire a landscape architect.

Pleaching

This is an old-world method of creating a living fence from trees instead of using shrubs. By planting trees close together and then intertwining their branches on a horizontal plane, a wall of branches, twigs and foliage will result.

The trees will grow best in full sun and generally will require adequate water. They should be spaced no more than four to five feet apart. If planted along a fence or strung wires, it makes for a more impenetrable barrier and will be easier to train the branches laterally. In the end, the tree barrier will pretty much obscure the fence.

There are many trees that can be used for pleaching, including willows, Russian olive, birch, beech, linden, and other fast growing trees. Pleaching is not for the impatient or those that need immediate protection. For a long-term solution it can be most effective and attractive.

Examples of Fences & Other Barriers

1. Wood Fence with Sheep Wire — 12' High
2. Tree Cage
3. Natural Hedge Fence
4. Tree Wrap
5. Electric Fence
6. Architecturally Designed Fence

Barriers Other than Fences

Many times a homeowner needs to protect trees or shrubs that may be outside a deer fenced area or may be specimen plants in an unfenced locale. Here are some methods of protection to consider. Most are simpler and less costly than securing a large area.

Tree Cages

Young trees are vulnerable to a deer's browsing habits, especially when they are relatively small and easily reached. This is particularly true of non-native trees not indigenous to your locale. All fruit trees and many flowering ornamentals are on a deer's tasty list.

A cage will protect a single tree, but it must be high enough to prevent a deer from reaching it when standing on its hind legs. It must also be installed wide enough to accommodate the trees natural spread, as it becomes tall enough to outgrow a deer's reach. The mesh should be small enough to prevent the deer from reaching through the mesh openings to grab a limb. If you are trying to protect a small orchard, then a conventional type deer fence is probably the desired option. If protecting a few trees, the barrier method is possibly the way to go. Here are some options.

Metal Post with Sheep Wire

Mark a square around your tree and remove any sod or weeds that may be there. Make the square large enough to accommodate future growth until the tree is of a size to no longer be deer feed or to the tree's ultimate size, if the fence is to be permanent. Set a metal post in each corner of your square and attach 6' mesh fencing with post clips. Attach one end in a manner that will allow easy removal at a later time as you may want to be able to enter the enclosure to weed or fertilize. It is not as important that the tree barrier be as tight to the ground as a regular fence, as it is unlikely a deer will crawl under the barrier into an enclosed area. Four inch mesh is an acceptable mesh size, but 2" is even more secure.

To reduce cost and labor you could set a single post and encircle the tree with the mesh wire. The other three sides can be held in place with short stakes. This is not quite as sturdy, but in most cases will deter a deer as well as the more substantial four stake method. When the mesh is no longer needed as a tree barrier, it can be moved to the vegetable garden and become an intensive method garden support. Set the circle of mesh in your garden and plant cucumbers, pole beans, peas or tomatoes around its perimeter. Put any garden debris and grass clippings inside the wire enclosure. This will keep weeds from growing. You have also effectively recycled your tree fence. Maybe you don't want to wait to recycle and should try this gardening method anyway?

Wooden Posts with Boards

This is the same concept as the previous fence. A wooden post with board fence is more substantial and will protect your tree against elk, horses, cattle and deer. It is more expensive, but also more attractive. Use treated posts or cedar for longevity. The fence can be kept natural looking or painted like the large horse farms in the east. The wood post and board fence is generally used when a permanent fence is desired. A post and pole fence works, but is generally not as strong.

Tree Wrap

Your tree may not be attractive to a deer's taste buds, but is still susceptible to bark damage from horn rubbings. By wrapping the trunk with a commercial tree wrap, you can avoid this problem and also protect the young tree from possible mice and vole bark chewing. Tree wrappings will also prevent winter sun scald, which can be a problem in some areas.

Tree Tubes

Tree tubes are not too well known and are relatively new devices for helping young trees get a start. From all reports they dramatically increase the growth and survival rates of young trees. They also prevent browsing and trunk damage.

Tree tubes are polypropylene tubes that are three, four or five feet tall. They are placed over a seedling at planting time. The seedling is forced to grow upward towards the light. The branches are contained within the tube. Check with your local extension service or arboretum regarding this method of protecting seedlings from damage and also enhancing growth.

Netting

There are various no-tangle soft nets that can be used to cover trees and other ornamentals. These are usually described as bird nets, but they can be used to protect new growth, strawberry patches, other berries, and fruits at harvest time. Don't spray edibles with most commercial deterrents.

Netting comes in a variety of widths and lengths and in various mesh sizes. It is usually green, which makes it virtually invisible. Deer just don't like to bite into netting. This can be a viable solution for temporary or seasonal protection. The netting can be used over many seasons, so it is fairly cost effective.

Protruding Wire Ends

I don't like this solution for many reasons, but I will present it because in some situations it has an application. Short wires can be tied to branches with the ends protruding. It is time consuming, somewhat dangerous to humans, but it will prevent deer from poking their nose into areas where you don't want them.

Row Covers

Floating row covers have been around for a long time. They have offered gardeners a way to protect their vegetable crops from the invasion of insects, as well as protecting crops against cool weather and frosts. Row covers also help retain moisture in the soil and moderate soil surface temperature. Light and water readily pass through the porous surface of the floating row covers. They also prevent deer from eating emerging plants. The row cover can actually be left on plants all season, as long as pollination is allowed and the row doesn't become too hot. Most gardeners use row covers only early in the season for their help in germination and for insect protection, but remove them later for appearance sake. Who wants to grow a bunch of white rows of fabric, when you should be looking at beautiful plants?

Similar to row covers, hoop houses can be constructed from one inch PVC pipe and covered with plastic sheeting.

Movable Deer Cages

If you are into raised beds you can make a mobile lightweight deer cage. If they are the usual 4' wide beds, make a light frame of wood and staple on 1" chicken wire. You can make it as high as that particular crop will grow or just make them 2' high, which will accommodate most vegetables.

If you are planting corn, make the cage four foot high and then use the intensive method of planting four kernels per square foot. Plant short height corn inside. Regardless of the height, you still need to make a screened top to prevent the deer from reaching inside.

Monofilament Fishing Line

This fence is practically invisible which will please the most discerning gardener. Use lightweight bamboo garden stakes and attach strong monofilament fishing line to it at four feet and two feet heights. This works if the deer are not too persistent.

A gardener in east central Florida insists that a monofilament fish line stretched taunt at a height of four feet will keep deer at bay. Dr. Dickman writing in American Rose Society magazine offers the conjecture that the taunt fishing line might vibrate at a frequency only heard by the deer.

6

Noisemakers

Sounds to confound! We know deer have acute hearing. We also know they are cautious, but curious. With these factors in place, just try to predict their behavior.

For all logical reasons, noisemakers should be effective, and at first, they generally are. Their effectiveness seems to diminish over a period of time. If you can disturb your deer enough initially to force them to change their habits of following a particular trail, you may have a winner. My only personal experience with noisemakers has been in rural areas, where deer have other feeding alternatives. Noisemakers have been known to alienate an entire neighborhood, both people and dogs. Suburbanites should probably consider ultrsonic devices.

I can report mixed results with these simple devices. Some claim great success and others only temporary relief.

Radios

When nighttime intrusion is the main problem, some folks claim playing a radio has wonderful results for scaring off all kinds of nocturnal visitors, including deer. Some go as far as claiming certain types of music are more effective than others. Once again you may have the problem of diminishing returns. Place your radio in a plastic bag for weather protection. Hope your neighbors aren't close for this one. Change its location from time to time.

Motion-Activated Sonic Warning

These devices emit a loud high-pitched sound that is well within a deer's hearing range. The device is programmed to change its sound and light pattern each time it is activated, so deer do not get used to the pattern. The combination of sudden light and sound seems to be a good combination.

Some of the devices monitor both body heat and motion of animals 50 feet away. Movement only monitors can search out even further.

These apparatuses can be either powered by your house current or powered by 9-volt batteries. They automatically turn off after each activation and reset themselves. Their very sensitivity can be a problem, as they can detect movement of animals as small as a mouse or a flying bat. This kind of activity could drive you or your neighbors crazy. Every time the thing activated and you look out the window expecting to see a deer, there will be nothing there because the mouse is already gone.

Motion-Activated Ultrasonic Warning

The ultrasonic warning device is similar to the sonic warning device, except it will make a sound like a loud car horn, but in a decibel level above the human range. These devices can sense activity in an area up to 4,000 square feet. They can be powered by either household current or solar power. Popular in suburban neighborhoods, they repel dogs as well as deer, with no offense to neighbors. The dog problem seems to be more acute in urban and suburban areas with dog owners letting their dogs run loose at night. It is less of a problem in rural areas, as a loose dog is at high risk of an early demise.

An ultrasonic warning device is an easy method to protect a relatively small area. It may also have the inherent problem of diminishing effectiveness. Some of these devices can be set for varying sensitivity and range. It is not for the inherently suspicious, for you cannot tell if the ultrasonic device is sounding off.

Thunder Guns

Thunder guns are used in Churchill, Manitoba to keep polar bears from overrunning the town in late summer and early fall. These non-projectile noisemakers are sometimes made available by local government agencies to protect alfalfa and grain fields. The thunder gun, used in the west, is programmed to fire automatically every 20 minutes. I have personally seen deer resting within 50 feet of a working thunder gun once it has been in operation for a period of time.

Firecrackers

Not a good solution! They have only a temporary effect and are generally illegal in most states. They can be dangerous and present a fire hazard. Don't use them.

Automotive Deer Whistles

To protect your car and yourself in areas of heavy deer populations, many drivers attach deer whistles to their front bumpers. These devices may either be sonic or ultrasonic. They are air movement activated and generally require speeds of 30 miles or more to be effective. There are other more expensive variations that are wired directly into your cars electrical system and will function at any speed.

Dusk and dawn are the two most vulnerable times. Observe deer crossing signs. They were put there for a reason. If a collision with a deer seems imminent, take your foot off the accelerator, brake lightly, but most importantly, keep a firm hold on the steering wheel, keeping the vehicle straight. Do not swerve in an attempt to miss the deer. Insurance adjusters claim more car damage and personal injury is caused by drivers attempting to avoid a collision and instead colliding with guard rails or rolling down grades.

Bamboo Flumes

Japanese gardens often feature a bamboo water flume that is decorative, interesting and a noisemaker that might help in the battle against deer. These bamboo flumes called shishi odoshi, literally meaning deer scarer. They work when water drips into a hollow bamboo tube. When the upper compartment fills with water it becomes heavier than the lower compartment and tips like a seesaw. The water drains out and the bottom falls back and clanks against a rock. If a heavy bamboo is used, the noise is quite loud and will startle deer — for a while.

Sight to cause flight! Deer have good eyesight and they are curious, but cautious. Maybe you can frighten them off using movement?

Shiny Objects

Some people tie plastic milk bottles, aluminum pie tins, colored flags or long streamers of colored yarn to fences or branches. These objects do identify the high point of a barrier, but unfortunately the deer generally acclimatize and they lose their effectiveness as visual "scare offs."

Artifical Predators

Plastic snakes, cutouts of hunters, cardboard dogs, cloth lions and bear skins have all been used to frighten deer. These things are fun and are good conversational pieces, but don't work in the long run. A live cheetah can be very effective on both deer and the mailman. Deer are the main diet of the Komodo dragons, a 12' monitor lizard that lives on Komodo Island in the Lesser Sundra Islands in Indonesia. They are hard to train.

Yard Nightlight

The motion of a sound-activated nightlight common to both farm yards and suburban areas initially will startle deer and cause them to leave the lighted area. However, they will remain in the dark recesses of your yard and eventually will not respond at all. Flashing lights seem to work better. This product was developed in the mountains of Maryland and is reportedly effective. A deer nightlight can be mounted on a barn, garage or house, or it can be attached to an electric fence or electric netting which will operate all night. If away from a power source, you may need a 12-volt battery or solar power.

Motion-Activated Lights

These flood lights are motion-activated and will stay on for 30 to 60 seconds. They too can be powered by household electricity, 12-volt battery or solar power. Most have sensitivity controls to prevent false alarms.

Water Spray Repellents

Here is a defense more kinetic than visual. This product is activated by a sensor and sprays bursts of water from a 360 degree adjustable head. It has a detection span field of 35 feet. It attaches to your garden hose and operates off two 9-volt batteries. Durable, easy-to-use, low cost and it works. Deer do not like this and they do not get used to it. People don't either.

Scary Eyes

These are round inflatables painted with large eyes. Some claim success against birds and deer as long as you move them.

8

Repellents — Home Remedies

Smell to repel! There are many repellents that can be formulated at home for a modest cost and sometimes from ingredients that are found around the home. They can be fairly effective for small area protection or to safeguard against specific plantings. Repellents work because their odor is repugnant to deer or the pungent taste is offensive to their bland taste preference.

The advantages of home remedies include low cost, easy application and no unsightly barriers. They do have their downside, such as the need to replenish after rains or long exposure to hot, dry or windy periods. If the mixture contains eggs, you will have to pour the mixture over the plant foliage instead of using a sprayer, as the egg coagulates and will clog the sprayer nozzle. Blood meal is an ingredient in some of these concoctions and can attract dogs and other carnivores. Putrid egg mixes seem to attract raccoons and the fats in soap are tasty to rodents. Most of the time these repellents will not be a cause for concern, but it is possible to create a new problem while trying to solve an old one.

Repellents need to be applied early in the growing season, before the deer begin to feed in the spring. It is much more difficult to dissuade them after their feeding patterns are established. The following are some tried and true remedies.

Human Hair

Hair is readily obtained from your local barber shop or beauty salon. Spread it around the base of the plant to be protected and at the drip line (the outside perimeter of the plant foliage). Human hair is protein and will gradually break down. Periodic replacement is necessary. Do not use treated hair.

Dog & Cat Hair

Dog and cat hair is obtainable from your local veterinarian or dog grooming parlor. Watch out for the fleas.

Blood Meal

Blood meal is used as a slow-release fertilizer and is available in small packages at nurseries and garden centers and in larger bags from farm supply stores. Blood meal, although a fertilizer, will not burn your plants. It can be spread at the base of your plants or mixed with water and sprayed on the foliage. A common method of application is to place three or four tablespoons of blood meal in a cheese cloth or nylon bag and tie onto the branches of the plants. If the plants cannot support the bags, then attach them to stakes driven into the ground near the plants. This method is double barreled in that it not only repels, but fertilizes as well. The blood meal must be replaced periodically, as it dries out or is leached away by rain.

Eggs, Soap & Pepper Mix

Mix raw eggs with liquid soap and hot cayenne pepper. The soap helps the mixture adhere to the foliage and has some repellent power of its own. The rotten egg smell is repugnant to a deer's sense of smell and the pepper is definitely offensive to its taste buds. Always test your mixture sparingly on a plant before making a wholesale application. Most of these mixtures have no toxic effects on most plants, but play it safe anyway.

Eggs & Onion Mix

This mixture is a variation of the standard egg, soap and pepper mix. Blend two eggs, including the shells, with two cups of chopped green onions, one tablespoon of fresh cayenne or chili powder and two cups of water. If you make too much, add some vinegar and oil and you have a fine marinade. A bit of garlic won't hurt either.

Eggs

Some rose growers report that applying a mixture of six eggs to one gallon of water will act as an effective repellent. Apply to the ground under the rose bushes as well as the stems and leaves. Remember to wash your cut roses before displaying them in the house, unless the sulfur smell is appealing to you. There is a small part of the general population that finds skunk smell appealing, so perhaps these are sulfur lovers also?

Old Socks

This is just a way to dispense any of the homemade concoctions. Soak your old socks (use the one the washer didn't eat) in the egg and pepper mix. Add some hair or blood meal or both to the mix. No soap is necessary. Attach the socks to branches or stakes. They are not very attractive, but novel. I wonder if it is the old socks or the repellent that offends the deer?

Gopher Purge

This is a biennial plant *(Euphorbia lathyris)* that supposedly keeps gophers from your garden and also repels the deer. I have not found it to be effective for stopping deer or gophers from performing their favorite pastime.

Gallon Holding Tanks

This is for the person that doesn't want to continually refresh their repellent. However, in dry country, evaporation will diminish the mix and in rainy parts of the country, continual rain will dilute it. Dig a hole in the ground to accommodate whatever size plastic container you propose to use as your holding tank. Place the jug in the hole, leaving $1/2$" of the lip protruding. Fill the container with a loose teepee of sticks. Replenish as needed.

Bar Soap

Tape Gold Dial soap into tree trunks, branches, fence posts or stakes. Some claim Irish Spring is preferable. Replace the bar as needed.

Soap Notes

A study conducted in Connecticut apple orchards revealed the key to successfully using soap to repel small numbers of deer was the distance between bars of soap. The researchers hung bars of Dial, Cashmere Bouquet, Ivory, Shield, Coast, Irish Spring, Safeguard, and Jergens from branches in the browse zone.

The distance between the bars was 2' to 6'. Damage was reduced by about 70% on branches located not more than 3' from the soap bars. There was no significant reduction on limbs located more than 3' from a bar. Soap apparently will not deter an entire herd, but will reduce damage if only a few deer are involved. You'll need a wholesale source for soap.

Some individuals still swear by certain brands based on their own experience. Perhaps there are regional differences? It may pay to experiment and stick with what works for you. Logic doesn't enter into this battle. Sometimes the easiest way to attach soap to the branches is to leave the paper covers on and drill a hole through the bar. The bar will last longer with the paper on and apparently is porous enough to still be effective. If the bar is foil wrapped, it's probably better to remove the foil covering. If you use twine to attach the soap, rather than wire, you will find it will not cut through the bar while hanging from the branch.

Most of these home remedies will work for part of a year, but sometimes fail to be effective later on. At other times they will work great for the entire year, but will not be as effective the next year. There really hasn't been enough scientific research done to understand all the nuances of what is happening. Perhaps changes in the weather, stress on the herd or availability of food are some of the factors affecting the effectiveness of these deterrents. You will have to make your own observations and draw your own conclusions. You are not the only one in your area with the problem. Talk to your neighbors and the local agencies regarding their success stories.

Human Urine

A while ago, *USA Today* had an interesting quote from Mike McGrath, then editor of *Organic Gardening* magazine. He was interviewed at the Philadelphia Flower Show about what he would do about deer. His reply was, "You have to mark your territory. You have to pee along your border. You have to get a carnivore to come over and pee around your garden if you're a vegetarian." This may work if you have a small garden, but it does have its limitations, unless you are a really big coffee drinker.

Scottish Deerhound Dogs

The origin of the deerhound breed is so obscure and of such antiquity that it is difficult to ascertain whether the Deerhound was at one time the same as the Irish Wolfdog (or Wolfhound) or whether over the course of centuries it was bred to be better suited to hunt the stags of Scotland.

So highly was the Deerhound held in esteem that it almost led to its demise due to restrictive breeding. The high value of the Deerhound was not only due to its relative scarcity, but also due to its prowess as a hunter. He has a very keen scent, great endurance, speed and strength, which was necessary coping with Scottish Deer, which often weighed 250 pounds. This dog craves human companionship, is quiet and dignified as well as being smart and alert. It is not aggressive, but has great courage and persistence. Dogs can certainly keep deer at bay. They can also chase them (bad news). Bark a lot (even worse news) and they seem to sleep a lot (the worse news). But if you opt for a dog, the Deerhound would be a more suitable family dog than Rottweilers or Wolfdogs.

Feeding Stations

This is not a fence, nor a repellent, but it is still an alternative. A woman in Damascus, Pennsylvania wrote me to say she has several acres under cultivation. She uses repellents in the spring on her gardens, but also feeds the deer year-round at a feeding station. She finds she is using less repellents each year. Many wildlife biologists, though, oppose this method as it can introduce diseases.

Commercial Repellents

There are a great number of commercial repellents on the market. Of course they are more expensive than their homemade counterparts. I have tried some and assume that they all work fairly well. Like the homemade mixes, they too must be replenished from time to time. I believe some will have a better adherence factor than the homemade varieties. You will find that the main ingredients in the commercial mixes are the same as your homemade variety — soap, pepper and eggs. They have the same advantages of little odor, no mess and easy to use. Some of the commercial repellents should not be applied to edibles 30 days before harvest. Always carefully read the label. All should be used in accordance with food agronomic practices.

The following lists the better-known deer repellents. More are being introduced each season, so check your local Ag. store or the Internet for the latest products. (See chapter 13 for more details)

Animal Get Away

Hot Pepper Wax
  Animal Repellent

BioDefend Deer Repellent

Liquid Fence Deer
  & Rabbit Repellent

Bobbex Deer Repellent

Miller Hot Sauce Animal
  Repellent

Chase Deer Repellent Spray

Nature's Defense
  Deer Repellent

Deer Away Deer and Rabbit

Not Tonight Deer! Repellent

Deer Ban Deer Repellent

Plant Pro-Tec Deer
  & Rabbit Garlic Units

Deer No No

Plant Saver All Natural
  Deer Repellent

Deer Off

ShotGun

Plantskydd Animal Repellent

Deer Pharm

Plotsaver Liquid Deer Repellent

Deer Scram — Deer
  & Rabbit Repellent

Repellex

Deerbusters Coyote Urine

Scoot Deer

Deerbusters Deer I Rotational
  Deer Repellent

Shake Away Animal Repellent

Deer Stopper

ShotGun Deer & Rabbit Repellent

Deervik

Hot Pepper Wax
  Animal Repellent

Green Screen Deer
  Repellent Bags

TerraCycle Deer Repellent

Hinder Deer & Rabbit
  Repellent

These and other repellents are offered through mail order catalogs and are available at local garden and farm supply retailers, as well as many mass merchandisers. Most are safe to use on your ornamentals, fruit trees, vegetables and flowers — provided the instructions are followed. Note: Some should not be used on edible plants. Check the label first. All should be tested on a small area on valuable plants that might be harmed by deer repellent products.

Most deer repellents work by either deterring because of a rank smell, bitter taste, predator scent, or a combination thereof. It is important to use deer repellent before deer start to browse and to change repellents frequently so that deer don't become familiar to one product or taste and adapt to it. Use a rotation of several different repellents throughout the season and change the location of the applications as well.

Many deer deterrents need to be applied frequently, especially after rain to keep the scents strong and effective (although some commercial products have good persistence for up to a month, even if it rains). Since deer have a wide browsing area, plants should be protected at least up to 6 feet from the ground or above the tallest snowbank. New growth on plants during the growing season also often requires repeat applications.

Strong scents that overwhelm deer will deter them because they become uncomfortable when they can't use their senses to smell danger. Also frequently effective are products that have an objectionable taste. Many commercial products are available that contain many of the following strong scents and tastes; putrescent eggs, capsaicin (chili peppers), garlic, onions, cloves, cinnamon, pepper, paprika, rosemary, wintergreen, peppermint or mint oil, acetic acid (vinegar), vitamin C and E, citrus and lemon extract, and mustard, fish or soybean oil.

Scented soaps with animal-based fatty acids also offer deer repellent abilities as well as hot pepper and wax products that taste bad and have a spicy deterrent.

Another group of deer deterrents contain products from predators (or that suggest predators are near). The smell of these bobcat, fox or coyote urine products triggers a response that a predator is nearby and deer take flight. Similarly, products with blood meal are used to give the impression that a predator is nearby and has recently killed prey.

Many homemade concoctions can be just as effective as commercial products at a fraction of the cost. The Internet is a good resource for homemade preparations. Look for recipes that include a little liquid dish detergent, vegetable oil, milk or white paint to help the spray "stick" to the plants. Once again, apply with caution to valuable plants and vegetables — test first and do not spray anything toxic on edible plants.

Whatever the product used, the key is to use several different types, reapply them as directed and apply them to different areas. Surprising deer with different tastes, smells, sights and sounds will startle and frighten them away from prized plants and gardens.

10

Deer & Plants

The following list of plants are generally not eaten by deer. As you already know, there is nothing sacred about what we claim to know about deer behavior. Deer will browse on any plant or just pull them out of the ground. I've witnessed this with a new planting of iris, when deer actually pulled a few out of the ground.

The lists in the following chapters were compiled from studies conducted by various conservation departments, county extension services, university agricultural departments, government agencies, master gardeners, nurseries, the guy next door and my own observations. Please don't take these lists as gospel, but the plants listed should generally fall into the categories as stated. The plants listed here are the more common varieties. If you have any experience with lesser known plants that fall into the "not preferred category," I would appreciate hearing from you. I am not a botanist or scientist and don't profess to know more about deer behavior or safe plants than any other dedicated observer. Hopefully, I may have collected a little more information than most, which I'm passing on with this book.

We do know that deer generally keep away from flowers or leaves that are spicy. They do not like aromatic or pungent foliage. Nor do they like fuzzy-leaved plants like lamb's ear. There are some plants and bulbs that are actually poisonous to deer if ingested in any quantity, such as foxglove. Somehow, they are aware of this and keep away from it. Prickly needles, spiny branches and thorns are all unpalatable. By combining the tangy with the bitter and the spicy with the prickly, you have a good start on creating a deer-proof garden.

Just as you think you know most of the answers regarding deer behavior, through your own careful observation, another piece will fall into the puzzle. You will find deer will sometimes browse plants that grow in the shade, but not in the sun.

Sometimes they will eat your neighbors plants, but not yours of the same species. What's the difference? Perhaps the make up of the soil, different fertilizers or even chemical insecticides? Apparently, obscure differences affect the way a plant tastes to a deer. Then again, is it merely chance that sends the deer to your garden and not next door? When they eat the plants growing in the shade but not the same species growing in the sun, is it they merely prefer the shade to stay cooler? Sometimes I think it's easy to try to read something into Bambi's behavior when it really is just a random happenchance.

We do know each season will affect a deers' eating habits. Spring, summer, fall and winter all present a different palette of culinary choices and different problems for the gardener and the deer.

Early Spring

The snow is gone if you live in northern climates, except in protected or shady areas. Below the snow line, the earth is beginning to show signs of a renewed life. Pregnant does particularly crave the green, easily digested tips of shrubs and trees and the newly emerging pasture grasses. If the wild forage has not yet burst forth, the emerging growth on your ornamentals is most appealing. They have just spent many months ingesting a less nutritional and less palatable diet, often full of low quality tannins. This is a vulnerable time. Stay alert.

The sappy new growth of certain tree species like maples, redbud and especially the weeping forms of fruit trees are particularly enticing. Fresh new lush grass is also attractive at this time of year. This browser will become a part-time grazer. Deer will slowly be moving to higher elevations in hill or mountain country. Elevation will somewhat determine when your spring arrives and also when the deer will return.

Summer

When a summer is particularly dry, a deer's taste will include succulents, which may not normally be on its diet list. It will also include berries and ripe fruit in an increasing amount. I've watched deer paw up ants and lick them up with their tongue. Did they like the moisture, taste, salts or minerals in the soil that may have attracted the ants in the first place?

Fall

Time to harvest. Better beat the deer to it if they're unprotected. Ripe corn, melons, squash; in fact most of your garden produce will be high on a deer's meal list. Apples, pears, plums and most other fruit are considered delicacies. The deer are fattening up for winter and the rut is about to begin. This is when those snorting bucks with raging hormones can do considerable damage to young trees and bushes.

Winter

This is the desperate time and the tips of trees, bushes and roses get nibbled away. Many times deer will descend from higher elevations into towns and create more havoc than they did in the other seasons.

Now to the list of plants deer usually avoid. I do have to emphasize *usually*, but these offer a good chance of avoiding deer damage. Plants not listed here, but in the same family are usually safe. Most wild flowers are safe and their cultivated cousins usually are as well. *Hortica: Color Cyclopedia of Garden Flora and Indoor Plants,* can provide the cross reference you need to find family relationships. This is a fabulous work, but expensive. Check your local library.

If you think your fancy imported tulips are pricey today, just look at this little tidbit from Charles Mackays' *Extraordinary Popular Delusions and the Madness of Crowds* about their value over 350 years ago.

> *How Much is Your Tulip Worth?* Two last of wheat; four tuns of beer; four last of rye; two tuns of butter; four fat oxen; one thousand pounds of cheese; eight fat swine; a suit of clothes; two hogsheads of wine; a silver drinking cup.

Plants Deer Usually Avoid

ANNUALS, BIENNIALS & PERENNIALS

BOTANICAL NAME	COMMON NAME (Cold Hardiness Zones)
Achillea	Yarrow (3)
Aconitum	Monkshood (2-4)
Ageratum	Floss Flower (9)
Aquilegia	Columbine (3)
Alstroemeria	Peruvian Lily (6)
Allium	Ornamental Onion (3-5)
Alcea	Hollyhock (3-5)
Aurinia	Basket of Gold Alyssum (3)
Ammi	False Queen Anne's Lace (8)
Amsonia	Bluestar (4-6)
Anemone	Anemone
Antirrhinum major	Snapdragon (7)
Arctotis	African Daisy (9)

Botanical Name	Common Name
Arisaema triphyllum	Jack-in-the-Pulpit (4-8)
Asclepias tuberosa	Butterfly Weed (4)
Astilbe	Astilbe (4)
Aubrietia	Rock Cress (4)
Bambusa	Clumping Bamboo (7)
Belamcanda	Blackberry Lily (5)
Bellis	English Daisy (4)
Begonia x semperflorens	Wax Begonia (9)
Bergenia	Bergenia (2-5)
Campanula	Bellflower (2-5)
Catananche	Cupid's Dart (4)
Centaurea	Bachelor's Button (2-5)
Echinacea	Coneflower (4)
Tanacetum coccineum	Painted Daisy (2-3)
Leucanthemum x superbum	Shasta Daisy (4)
Chrysanthemum	Chrysanthemum (3-5)
Actaea	Bugbane (4)
Consolida	Larkspur (7)
Coreopsis	Tickseed (6-8)
Cosmos	Cosmos (8)
Crocus	Crocus (4-6)
Dahlia	Dahlia (8)
Datura	Thorn Apple (8)
Delphinium	Delphinium (3)
Dianthus caryophyllus	Carnation (4)
Dianthus	Pinks (2)
Dianthus barbatus	Sweet William (2)

Botanical Name	Common Name
Dicentra	Bleeding Heart (3)
Digitalis	Foxglove (4)
Echinops	Globe Thistle (2)
Epimedium	Epimedium (4)
Erica	Heath (5)
Fritillaria imperialis	Crown Imperial (4)
Gaillardia	Blanket Flower (3)
Helleborus	Hellebore (4-6)
Heliotropium arborescens	Heliotrope (9)
Hypoestes phyllostachya	Polka Dot Plant (9)
Iberis sempervirens	Candy Tuft (3)
Ipomoea	Morning Glory (7)
Lavandula	Lavender (4-7)
Leucojum	Snowflake (5)
Lilium lancifolium	Tiger Lily (2)
Limonium latifolium	Statice (2)
Linaria	Toadflax (4)
Linum perenne	Blue Flax (4)
Lobelia erinus	Lobelia (9)
Lobularia maritima	Sweet Alysum (8)
Lupinus	Lupine (3-4)
Lychnis chalcedonica	Maltese Cross (2)
Lychnis coronaria	Rose Campion (3)
Lysimachia	Loosestrife (4)
Matthiola	Stock (6)
Matricaria	Chamomile (4-8)
Matteuccia	Ostrich Fern (1)

Botanical Name	Common Name
Mentha pulegium	Penny Royal (8)
Mirabilis jalapa	Four O'Clock (8)
Monarda didyma	Beebalm (3)
Muscari	Grape Hyacinth (4)
Myosotis	Forget-Me-Not (3)
Narcissus	Daffodil (4-6)
Narcissus	Narcissus (4-6)
Nigella	Love-In-The-Mist (8)
Oenothera	Evening Primrose (3)
Paeonia	Peony (2-4)
Papaver	Poppy (2-6)
Pelargonium x hortorum	Geranium (9)
Physalis	Chinese Lantern (2)
Platycodon grandiflorus	Balloon Flower (3)
Rudbeckia	Blackeyed Susan (2-5)
Salvia	Sage (3-8)
Sedum	Sedum (2-3)
Centaurea cineraria	Dusty Miller (7)
Sempervivum	Hens and Chickens (1)
Silybum	Thistle (7)
Stokesia	Stokes Aster (5)
Stachys byzantina	Lamb's Ear (3)
Tanacetum	Tansy (4)
Tagetes	Marigold (9)
Trollius	Globeflower (3)
Verbena	Verbena (7)
Viola	Violet (4)

Botanical Name	Common Name
Yucca	Yucca (2-5)
Zinnia	Zinnia (9)

My personal experience has been to plant Aquilegia (columbine) as a safe plant, but many master gardeners do not agree and report it to be highly susceptible to deer damage. I'm sure there are other differences in opinion regarding other plants on my "safe" list as well. As a caution, I cannot emphasize enough the need to test plants before you do extensive plantings. I do believe you'll have a 90% success rate if you stay with plants on this list. As mentioned before, many other plants in the same family as these deer-proof plants will also be safe.

TREES

BOTANICAL NAME	COMMON NAME (Cold Hardiness Zones)
Alnus	Alder (2)
Betula	Birch (2)
Carpinus	Hornbeam (3)
Castanea	Chestnut (4)
Catalpa	Catalpa (4)
Cedrus	Cedar (7)
Cercis	Redbud (4)
Cladrastis	Yellowwood (4)
Cornus	Dogwood (2-7)
Corylus	Hazel (4)
Cupressus	Cypress (7)
Elaeagnus angustifolia	Russian Olive (3)
Fagus	Beech (4)

Botanical Name	Common Name
Fraxinus	Ash (4)
Gleditsia	Honey Locust (3)
Laburnum	Golden Chain Tree (5)
Larix	Larch (2)
Liquidambar	Sweetgum (6)
Liriodendron	Tulip Tree (6)
Magnolia	Magnolia (5)
Morus	Mulberry (5)
Picea	Spruce (3)
Quercus	Oak (3-7)
Rhus	Sumac (2)
Robinia	Black Locust (5)
Sorbus	Mountain Ash (2)
Tsuga	Hemlock (3)

The blue spruce and other varieties of the spruce family tree are widely grown as ornamentals. Fortunately, this is one of the few conifers on the deer safe list, at least in the West.

HERBS

BOTANICAL NAME	COMMON NAME (Cold Hardiness Zones)
Allium schoenoprasum	Chives (3)
Anethum	Dill (8)
Borago	Borage (7)
Coriandrum	Coriander (8)
Cuminum	Cumin (8)

Botanical Name	Common Name
Foeniculum	Fennel (8)
Lavandula	Lavender (4-7)
Mentha	Mint (3)
Origanum	Oregano (6)
Pimpinella	Anise (8)
Petroselinum crispum	Parsley (5)
Rosmarinus	Rosemary (7)
Rumex	Sorrel (4)
Salvia	Sage (3-8)
Sassafras	Sassafras (4)
Satureja	Savory (5)
Symphytum	Comfrey (4)
Tanacetum	Tansy (4)
Thymus	Thyme (5)

A deer's preference for a bland taste makes herb gardening a viable choice. I would guess that any other pungent herb, even if not listed here, would be a safe choice. For example, I have no experience with bay laurel, but would think it is deer proof.

VINES

BOTANICAL NAME	COMMON NAME (Cold Hardiness Zones)
Bignonia	Cross Vine (6)
Ipomoea	Moon Flower (7)
Campsis	Trumpet Creeper (6)
Celastrus	Bittersweet (4)
Clematis	Clematis (2-6)

Botanical Name	Common Name
Cissus	Grape Ivy (9)
Ipomoea	Morning Glory (7)
Lonicera	Honeysuckle (3-7)
Parthenocissus tricuspidata	Boston Ivy (4)
Ipomoea quamoclit	Cypress Vine (8)
Wisteria	Wisteria (6)
Vitis	Grape (3)

This should be a safe list, but I've seen Clematis heavily damaged and grape leaves on an arbor totally destroyed up to 6' high. My Boston Ivy has never been eaten, but I've had reports of ivy as a favorite lunchtime snack. When you read other safe lists, you'll see everyone is not in agreement.

GROUND COVERS

BOTANICAL NAME	COMMON NAME (Cold Hardiness Zones)
Aegopodium podagraria	Bishop's Weed (3)
Convallaria majalis	Lily of the Valley (4)
Pachysandra	Pachysandra (4)
Vinca minor	Periwinkle (3)

Vinca minor is another case of mixed reports from perfectly safe to "hungrily devoured." I suspect the varying reports may have to do with the age of the plantings or their location.

SHRUBS

BOTANICAL NAME	COMMON NAME (Cold Hardiness Zones)
Berberis	Barberry (3)
Buddleja davidii	Butterfly Bush (5)
Caragana	Pea Shrub (2)
Cotinus	Smoketree (4)
Forsythia	Forsythia (4)
Ligustrum	Privet (5-7)
Mahonia	Oregon Grape (6)
Philadelphus	Mock Orange (5)
Potentilla	Potentilla (2-4)
Symphoricarpos	Snowberry (2)
Syringa vulgaris	Lilac (2)
Vaccinium	Blueberry (2)

Lilacs are generally safe as they mature, but should be protected when young. I have not had any experience with *Euonymus alata* (Burning Bush), but I believe it to be in the safe category.

VEGETABLES

BOTANICAL NAME	COMMON NAME (Cold Hardiness Zones)
Allium cepa	Onions (3)
Brassica oleracea var. italica	Broccoli (8)
Brassica oleracea var. gemmifera	Brussel Sprouts (8)
Brassica oleracea var. capitata	Cabbage (8)
Brassica oleracea var. botrytis	Cauliflower (8)

Botanical Name	Common Name
Brassica campestris var. pekinensis	Chinese Cabbage (8)
Brassica oleracea var. acephala	Collards (8)
Brassica oleracea var. acephala	Kale (7)
Brassica juncea	Mustard Greens (8)
Lepidium sativum	Cress (7)
Fragaria	Strawberry (5)
Rheum	Rhubarb (3)

The hairier the strawberry leaves, the safer the plant will be. This is true of all plants on this list. The stronger the taste, the fuzzier the leaves, the pricklier the stems, the safer the plant.

Plants Deer Occasionally Eat

The following plants are not high on the deers' gourmet list, but in times of drought or if other food is not available, these plants will be browsed. Viola, for example, is considered feeding frenzy food in some areas. I personally have not found that to be true.

ANNUALS, BIENNIALS & PERENNIALS

BOTANICAL NAME	COMMON NAME (Cold Hardiness Zones)
Achimenes	Orchid pansy (8)
Helianthus	Sunflower (8)
Viola	Violet, Pansy (4)

TREES

BOTANICAL NAME	COMMON NAME (Cold Hardiness Zones)
Acer saccharinum	Silver Maple (3)
Cornus	Dogwood (2-7)
Aesculus hippocastanum	Horsechestnut (3)
Magnolia soulangiana	Saucer Magnolia (4)
Pyrus communis	Pear (4)
Syringa reticulata	Japanese Tree Lilac (3)
Tilia americana	Basswood (4)
Tsuga	Hemlock (3)

SHRUBS

BOTANICAL NAME	COMMON NAME (Cold Hardiness Zones)
Cotinus	Smoketree (4)
Forsythia	Forsythia (4)
Hamamelis	Witch Hazel (5)
Philadelphus	Mock Orange (5)
Rosa rugosa	Rugosa Rose (3)
Viburnum	Viburnum (4-6)

The following is a list of plants that deer absolutely love. Many are the mainstay of every vegetable garden and many are our all-time favorite flowers for the border and cutting. Most of our fruit trees are on the list. The ornamentals that are not native seem to be particularly vulnerable, but "going native" is not a sure bet either. As mentioned earlier, all these lists are merely guides and sometimes local gardeners report different results. There are so many factors that enter into the safeness formula. The size of the herd, territory open to movement, overall deer population density, availability of natural forage, the time of the year and weather conditions all enter into the unpredictability and complexity of the deers' eating habits. Don't be too confused by seeing the same plant in several lists. This merely confirms the different opinions among "experts," including myself. There is not much disagreement about the Plants Deer Love list.

Plants Deer Love
ANNUALS, BIENNIALS, PERENNIALS

BOTANICAL NAME	COMMON NAME (Cold Hardiness Zones)
Alcea rosea	Hollyhock (4)
Chrysanthemum	Chrysanthemum (3-5)
Crocus	Crocus (4-6)
Hemerocallis	Daylily (3)
Hosta	Hosta (2)
Impatiens	Impatiens (9)
Lilium	Lily (2-4)
Lobelia cardinalis	Cardinal Flower (4)
Phlox	Phlox (4)
Rosa	Rose (3-7)
Trillium	Trillium (2-5)
Tulipa	Tulip (4)
Viola	Violet (4)

These are some of the plants most often being reported as deer fodder. Check with your county extension service, local master gardeners, nurseries and best of all, your neighbors. You'll find even more plants than listed here.

TREES

BOTANICAL NAME	COMMON NAME (Cold Hardiness Zones)
Abies balsamea	Balsam Fir (3)
Acer platanoides	Norway Maple (4)
Cercis canadensis	Eastern Redbud (4)
Cornus mas	Cornelian Dogwood (4)
Malus	Apple (4)
Prunus	Cherry (5)
Prunus	Plums (5)
Fraxinus excelsior	European Ash (4)
Kalmia latifolia	Mountain Laurel (4)
Malus	Crabapple (4)
Salix	Willow (2-6)

SHRUBS

BOTANICAL NAME	COMMON NAME (Cold Hardiness Zones)
Hydrangea	Hydrangea (4-7)
Rhododendron	Rhododendron (5-7)
Rhododendron	Azalea (3-7)
Syringa patula	Korean Lilac (3)
Thuja	Arborvitae (5)

VINES

BOTANICAL NAME	COMMON NAME (Cold Hardiness Zones)
Lathyrus odoratus	Sweet Pea (8)
Parthenocissus tricuspidata	Boston Ivy (4)

VEGETABLES

BOTANICAL NAME	COMMON NAME (Cold Hardiness Zones)
Cucumis sativus	Cucumber (8)
Curcurbita maxima	Winter Squash (8)
Curcurbita pepo	Summer Squash (8)
Curcurbita pepo	Pumpkin (8)
Lactuca sativa	Lettuce (8)
Solanum lycopersicum	Tomato (8)
Solanum tuberosum	Potato (8)
Zea mays	Corn (8)

Plants That are Harmful to Humans When Eaten

Flowering bulbs are potentially dangerous and some seeds and leaves are also harmful to humans when eaten. Some of these are also repugnant to deer.

Angel's Trumpet	Jack-in-the-Pulpit	Potato
Belladonna	Jimsonweed	Ragwort
Bleeding Heart	Laburnum	Rosary Pea
Bracken Fern	Lantana	Skunk Cabbage
Castor Bean	Lobelia	Squirrel Corn
Celandine	Larkspur	Snow-on-the-Mountain
Christmas Rose	Lily-of-the-Valley	Star-of-Bethlehem
Cocklebur	Marsh Marigold	Stinging Nettle
Deadly Nightshade	Mayapple	Tobacco
Delphinium	Monkshood	Vetch
Dogbane	Moonseed	Water Hemlock
Elderberry	Oleander	White Snakeroot
Foxglove	Poison Hemlock	Wisteria
Groundsel	Poison Ivy	Wolfbane
Henbane	Poison Oak	Yew
Horse Nettle	Poison Sumac	
Horsechestnut	Pokeweed	
Iris	Poppies	

The above list is from the Poisonious Plants Informational Database, Cornell University *www. ansci.cornell.edu/ plants/index.html*.

Lyme Disease

Deer damage is one problem, but Lyme disease is truly a growing concern that can result in a serious medical condition. Lyme disease was first diagnosed in Connecticut over thirty years ago. It slowly moved westward, resulting in a fairly high incident of the disease in Wisconsin. By the mid-1990's it had reached eastern Washington state and continues to move toward the Pacific.

Lyme disease is caused by a bacteria which is transmitted by the bite of the blacklegged or deer tick *(Ixodes scapularis)*. Because these ticks are very small, many times they will go undetected. The preferred habitat of the deer tick are wooded areas, adjacent pastures and open areas enjoyed by deer. The tick is spread in the wild by many other animals too, including rodents and birds.

The ticks' bite is not painful and seldom noticed. If the tick is carrying Lyme disease, in most cases, the early symptom will be a slowly spreading circle of rash. At other times, the rash will be confined to a ring around the bite area. After several days, the rash will disappear. Along with the rash, the patient often suffers fatigue, headache, stiff neck, stiffness in the joints or muscles and a swelling of the joints.

In locations where Lyme disease is not prevalent, it is sometimes misdiagnosed. The untreated progression of the illness goes from the rash stage to the symptoms mentioned above and ultimately to arthritic, cardiac or neurological disorders, and even death. This is a serious disease, but one that can be treated effectively in its early stages.

Now What?

As I've previously mentioned, I have not tried all the defensive measures mentioned in this book. At least I do have credentials based on longevity and determination. I have fought the deer war from upstate New York, throughout the Boston area, down to Maryland and North Carolina, then back up through the midwest of Chicagoland and Minneapolis. I'm now gardening in eastern Washington state and the war continues. If losing many battles in my fifty years of confrontation makes me an expert, then I am pre-eminently qualified.

Some of the answers to your problems and the solutions provided are almost 100% foolproof, but they may not be economically prudent, aesthetically attractive or may be too labor intensive. Others may require too much after application attention or maintenance. Some of the answers suggested may be less than perfect, but are acceptable for your situation. Most often you will need to incorporate more than one solution.

If your temperament does not allow you to go to war, then the obvious solution is to identify enough plants that deer generally avoid in your area. If you choose this direction, you have just become the winner of the deer wars. You can expand the list noted on these pages by consulting *Hortica* to determine what plants exist in the same family of proven deer-resistant plants. You can also obtain information from The American Horticulture Society located in Alexandria, Virginia at their website *www.ahs.org*. The directory lists hundreds of horticultural societies. Some are state organizations and some are for specific interests, such as the American Rose Society. These organizations might be able to help you compile your list of deer-proof plants for your area. There are several books written listing deer-resistant plants. *Deer Resistant Ornamentals for the Northern States* by Pamela Gehn Stephens and *Gardening in Deer Country* by Karen Bernard. Cornell University also provides a much used list. Some nurseries such as Green Gardens in Oregon, provide their own list of safe plants, at least safe in their area.

On my twenty acres, located in remote mountain country, there is a heavy population of whitetails, mule deer, a small herd of elk, with a roaming moose or two thrown in for good measure. Thus my lifelong battle continues with new rules and clever adversaries. "I have seen yesterday, I love today and I am not afraid of tomorrow." I have bested my foe, but it wasn't easy. Here are the several defensive measures I had to deploy to keep my sanity and my plants. I am too stubborn and not sensible enough to try to co-exist. My deer are now much dearer to my heart. I have about five acres of my twenty acre homestead under some kind of cultivation. As it was not economically feasible for me to construct a 10' deer fence around the entire area, I was forced to incorporate a variety of methods.

A thirty tree orchard is protected with a 10' high deer fence, This barrier was built prior to planting the trees. No problem here. The fence is constructed of 12' treated western larch 4" x 4" posts, strung with 4" mesh sheep wire. The orchard is on fairly level ground, so the wire comes down close to the bottom of the posts, alleviating the need for any ground barrier. My wooden gate is 6' wide and only 7' high. Thus far, no deer has jumped over the gate.

A 50' x 100' vegetable garden is also protected with a similar fence. Incidentally, although we are located close to the Canadian border, we also overlook the Columbia River. This provides a warm micro climate that prevents the posts from frost heaving, although they are only 2' in the ground. However, each corner post is set in concrete and corner bracing is also used. The vegetable garden fence has a 2' chicken wire mesh along the bottom of the fence. This effectively keeps grouse, rabbits, ground squirrels, skunks and other critters from entering the garden.

These two fenced areas are connected with a 30' grape arbor. Each of the eight climbing grape vines had to be protected with a 6' wire cage. Once the grape vines reached the top of the arbor, the cages were removed.

A 30' x 50' formal rose garden is enclosed on three sides with a Chinese elm hedge. This was protected with an egg, pepper, blood meal spray when it was young. It was my understanding that once the hedge reached maturity it would be relatively deer proof. Not so. One side became a grazing picnic, which destroyed the formal look we were trying to attain.

The fourth side of the rose garden is an arbor covered with thorny climbing roses. Apparently they were not thorny enough, because late in the season, the deer actually entered through the arbor entrance and feasted on the tea roses inside. These raids, usually at night, led to the final solution.

Along the roadway, coming up to the house, is a 60' long rock garden. The garden is cut into the side of a bank and is planted primarily with succulents such as sedum and sepervivum. They survived for years untouched, until one particularity dry year the moisture filled plants were discovered. Within a few weeks the entire bed was devastated. Fortunately, these plants are tough to kill and due to the deer's dental arrangement with no top front teeth, they couldn't eat the entire low growing plant, although some would be found uprooted. With some replanting and a little extra water, the bed rejuvenated the next year and is now flourishing. It was interesting to note that this attraction to the rock garden was from one old doe. The younger deer with fawns did not seem interested.

This same hot, dry, fire threatening year also saw attacks on the perennial and annual beds close to the house. In prior years these areas were sacrosanct. The deer had not ventured that close to the house in previous years, but the extremely dry weather changed their patterns. Up to this time I thought we had drawn truce lines and I was willing to share a little. I finally realized there is no honor with a hungry deer.

First the rose garden, then the rock garden, and now the perennial beds. This prompted the decision to fence a two-acre perimeter around the house. We live near the nation's largest National Forest, so it was not difficult to obtain a permit to cut wood from the slack piles in the timbered areas. We cut 500 six foot long 4" to 6" fir posts. It took several trips to haul them home. The slack piles were several years old, so the posts peeled relatively easy. Digging the post holes and setting them went fairly fast, with my digging and my wife, Elaine, setting. I used the double fence method with chicken wire and attached an outrigger wire on the bottom posts 18" from the ground on the deer's side (outside).

On our side (inside), we planted a caragana hedge, spaced every three feet. The bushes were available from our conservation department at nominal cost. As the caragana grew, it completely enveloped the unsightly chicken wire fence. The barrier is definitely deer proof and may be even reaching bear proof status. There are still some ornamental and specimen trees planted outside the fenced areas. These are individually caged while we wait for them to grow tall enough to be beyond the deer's browsing height.

Fifty young walnut trees are also outside the fenced area. The local nursery from whom we purchased the seedlings assured us walnut trees are deer proof. We were cautious and covered each small tree with a 3' cage of chicken wire. Some of the trees have grown out of their protective cages and were not bothered by the deer. In retrospect, the cages were a detriment. The bear cubs seem to delight in smashing the cages, which also damages the trees at times. We've put walnut trees on our safe list.

There is another small garden outside the perimeter fenced area. This is protected with a three-strand electric fence. Remember the peanut butter! This is only a 4' high fence, but the nose buzz keeps them away. It almost seems they can sense the electric current, but on the other hand when I forget to plug it in at times, they still don't come near it, if they have already been conditioned. I rejected using an electric fence for the entire perimeter area for two reasons. First, this is very dry country in the summer and I worried about potential fire danger (probably unwarranted). Second, I did not want to see an extensive fencing around our entire garden area, so I preferred putting in the effort to install a fence that would ultimately become a hedge. I am also retired and have the pleasure of unstructured time and good health.

To protect some of the hedges early on, I used homemade pepper spray concocted from a mixture of pepper, soap and eggs. At times I added blood meal, if it was on hand. This was effective as long as I replaced it at intervals.

To protect my gardens, I am using deterrent sprays, different kinds of barrier fences, an electric fence, cages and hedges. We are now secure. You, too, can find the right combination of systems to help protect your plants and gardens in deer country. Although I have never personally used the netting systems, the reports from those that used them seem favorable. The best part of a protected garden is the enjoyment of deer as beautiful animals, instead of dreadful predators of your garden. They will become much more endearing when they are not dining on your roses, but are over at the neighbors having dinner. We are now able to sit on our decks and watch the many deer without feeling apprehensive about our gardens. This is a nice feeling.

It's your choice! You can choose to fight an all out war and never surrender, or you can choose to live more peacefully, but with some protection and share part of your bountiful garden, or the third choice of planting only deer-resistant plants. If you choose the third alternative, you'll probably have to forget about tea roses, daylilies, some vegetables and don't even try tulips. What you will achieve is I.P. (inner peace).

Good Luck! Fighting the deer wars can be humbling, frustrating, infuriating, but also rewarding as you become to know this fascinating animal better. You, too, can lose enough battles to become a qualified expert, if you live as long as I have. Here's the good news. We don't have to deal with herds of feral goats. They really do eat everything.

There are many sources for the products mentioned in this book. In addition to nurseries, discount stores, garden centers and farm stores.

When looking for fencing materials, check around at the various lumber yards and farm centers. Prices can vary considerably. Investigate recycle depots, demolition sites and farms being converted to suburban development. Sometimes you can get lucky and obtain free or low cost materials.

Product Name: Deer Off

Type: Odor and Taste?

Product Formulation: RTU & Conc.

Active Ingredient(s): Putrescent eggs, capsaicin and garlic

Manufacturer: Woodstream Corporation, 69 North Locust Street, Lititz, PA 17543 Phone: 717-626-2125

Website: *www.woodstreamcorp.com*

Description: Deer Off is an all-natural, environmentally friendly deer repellent that is easy to apply, not harmful to humans, animals or the environment. The solution produces an odor and taste that is offensive to animals but mild enough not to bother humans. This highly effective food-based product deters deer from browsing on valuable ornamental plants, flowers, shrubs and trees.

Product Name: Plantskydd Animal Repellent

Type: Predator Fear **Product Formulation:** Granular/Powder, RTU & Conc.

Active Ingredient(s): Dried blood meal, processed animal protein, vegetable fat and salt

Manufacturer: American Protein Corporation, 1 Vision Aire Place, Suite 2, Ames IA 50010 Phone: 800-252-6051

Website: *www.plantskydd.com*

Description: Plantskydd Deer Repellent has a vegetable oil binder to stick to plants for up to 6 months over winter or 3-4 months in summer. Plantskydd works by emitting an odor that animals associate with predator activity stimulating a fear-based response which will repel deer.

Certified Organic: Yes

Product Name: Deer No No

Type: Odor

Product Formulation: RTU

Active Ingredient(s): Soap-sodium salts of mixed fatty acids and citrus.

Manufacturer: Deer No No Inc 186 Dibble Hill Road, West Cornwall, CT 06796 Phone: 203-672-6264

Website: *www.deernono.com*

Description: Deer No No is citrus based and is hung on trees every 2 feet at deer browsing level. The green net bags can be hung from branches or attached to a stake and placed in the soil around plants. Deer No No is effective for 10 to 12 months.

Product Name: Hinder Deer & Rabbit Repellent

Type: Odor

Product Formulation: Conc. & RTU

Active Ingredient(s): Ammonium soaps of higher fatty acids

Manufacturer: Amvac Chemical Corporation, 4100 E. Washington Blvd. Los Angeles, CA 90023-4406 Phone: 888-462-6822

Website: *www.amvac-chemical.com*

Description: Hinder Deer Repellent builds a fence of odor that helps protect against damage from deer and rabbits. It remains effective for up to 4 weeks and should be reapplied every 3 weeks. The active ingredient is not harmful to pets when used as directed.

Product Name: ShotGun Deer & Rabbit Repellent

Type: Taste & Odor

Product Formulation: Conc. & RTU

Active Ingredient(s): Putrescent egg, garlic and capsaicin

Manufacturer: Bonide Products, Inc. 6301 Sutliff Road, Oriskany, NY 13424 Phone: 800-424-9300

Website: *www.bonideproducts.com*

Description: ShotGun Deer & Rabbit Repellent protects flowers, shrubs, vegetables, fruit, bulbs, lawns and trees from deer, rabbits and squirrels by using both an odor and a taste barrier. It contains all natural ingredients, lasts 3 months and leaves no noticeable residue.

Product Name: ShotGun Hot Pepper Wax Animal Repellent

Type: Taste & Odor

Product Formulation: Conc. & RTU

Active Ingredient(s): Capsaicin

Manufacturer: Bonide Products, Inc. 6301 Sutliff Road, Oriskany, NY 13424 Phone: 800-424-9300

Website: *www.bonideproducts.com*

Description: ShotGun Hot Pepper Wax Animal Repellent is a natural repellent for use on fruits, vegetables and ornamentals. It even stops animals from chewing wood structures and fences. One application can last up to 4 weeks.

Product Name: ShotGun Repels-All

Type: Taste & Odor

Product Formulation: Conc. & RTU

Active Ingredient(s): Dried blood, putrescent eggs, garlic oil, clove, fish oil, onion, and wintergreen

Manufacturer: Bonide Products, Inc. 6301 Sutliff Road, Oriskany, NY 13424 Phone: 800-424-9300

Website: *www.bonideproducts.com*

Description: ShotGun Repels-All is made with all natural ingredients but repulsive to vermin and other undesirables. It repels three ways, by sense of touch, taste and smell. It protects plants and property, including structures, for up to 2 months per application. ShotGun Repels-All is rain fast after 6 hours and safe to use around edibles.

Product Name: Hot Pepper Wax Animal Repellent

Type: Taste

Product Formulation: RTU

Active Ingredient(s): Capsaicin, hot cayenne peppers, food-grade paraffin wax

Manufacturer: Hot Pepper Wax, Inc, 305 Third Street, Greenville, PA 16125 Phone: 724-646-2300

Website: *www.hotpepperwax.com*

Description: Hot Pepper Wax is made from a concentrate of cayenne peppers, assorted repelling herbs and food grade paraffin wax. Mix it with water and spray. It stays on the plant for up to three weeks with no need to apply after every rainfall or watering. The natural wax also offers protection to plants from hot, dry and windy conditions. Food plants do not absorb the heat of the pepper and the wax washes off easily with warm water.

Product Name: Chase Deer Repellent Spray

Type: Taste

Product Formulation: RTU

Active Ingredient(s): Pepper Oil

Manufacturer: Preferred Products Inc, 8459 US Highway 42, Suite 278, Florence, KY 41042 Phone: 859-525-7353

Website: *www.chase-mole.com/pages/products/deer.html*

Description: Stop deer from using your yard as a salad bar! Chase Deer Repellent spray uses taste and smell to discourage browsing deer. Spray plants with this all-natural product to keep deer away from your valuable shrubs, trees and flowers. Chase Deer Repellent won't wash off and leaves no residue. Works up to 3 months and is safe for people, pets and the environment.

Product Name: Plant Pro-Tec Deer & Rabbit Garlic Units

Type: Taste & Odor

Product Formulation: RTU

Active Ingredient(s): Oil of garlic; capsaicin and related Capsaicinoids

Manufacturer: Plant Pro-Tec, P.O. Box 902, Palo Cedro, CA 96073 Phone/Fax: 530-547-5450

Website: *www.plantprotec.com*

Description: Plant Pro-Tec Garlic Units discourage deer, elk and rabbits from destroying plants in lawns and gardens. They are effective and long-lasting for 6 to 8 months. Easy to use — just break a barrier and clip to a plant or fence. Plant Pro-Tec is safe with a 100% organic formulation and biodegradable plastic container.

Product Name: Repellex Deer & Rabbit Repellent

Type: Taste & Odor

Product Formulation: Conc. & RTU

Active Ingredient(s): Dried animal blood, paprika concentrate, pepper and garlic oils.

Manufacturer: Repellex USA Inc. P.O. Box 396, Niles, MI 49120 Phone: 877-737-3539

Website: *www.repellex.com*

Description: Repellex Deer and Rabbit is a repellent that is designed to bind and stick to woody and leafy surfaces of flowers and ornamentals for up to 90 days of protection. Repellex is a natural repellent that is safe to use. For best results, reapply throughout the season when new growth is present. Repellex does have a noticeable smell when applied which will subside within 24-48 hours of application.

Product Name: Deerbusters Coyote Urine

Type: Predator Fear

Product Formulation: RTU

Active Ingredient(s): Coyote urine

Manufacturer: Deerbusters, 9735A Bethel Road, Frederick, MD 21702 Phone: 888-422-3337

Website: *www.deerbusters.com*

Description: Deerbusters Coyote Urine is a 100 percent urine lure that creates the illusion that predators are present in the area. It is great for photographers, gardeners, hunters and wildlife enthusiasts. Using predator urine give deer and other animals the illusion of a predator in the area causing them to give your area a wide berth.

Product Name: Dial Bar Soap

Type: Odor

Product Formulation: RTU

Active Ingredient(s): Fragrance, fatty acids, etc.

Manufacturer: The Dial Corporation, 15101 N Scottsdale Road, Scottsdale, AZ 85254-9934 Phone: 800-258-3425

Website: *www.dialsoap.com*

Description: Dial Soap can be used as a deer repellent. Just drill a hole through each bar and hang one in each tree.

Product Name: Bobbex Deer Repellent

Type: Taste & Odor

Product Formulation: Conc. & RTU

Active Ingredient(s): Garlic oil, acetic acid, cloves, gelatin, fish meal, edible fish oil, onions, eggs, vanillin, wintergreen oil, and vitamins C and E

Manufacturer: Bobbex Inc, 52 Hattertown Road, Newtown, CT 06470 Phone: 1-800-792-4449

Website: *www.bobbex.com*

Description: Systematic use of Bobbex Deer Repellent will substantially reduce damage to plantings by interrupting the browsing habits of deer, which are turned away by its taste and odor. Bobbex at the same time is a nutritional product providing ingredients which favorably increase plant vitality and vigor.

Product Name: Not Tonight Deer!

Type: Taste & Odor

Product Formulation: Repellent Powder

Active Ingredient(s): Dehydrated whole egg solids and white pepper

Manufacturer: Not Tonight Deer! 428 West Spruce Lane, Louisville, CO 80027 Phone: 888-535-2030

Website: *www.nottonight.com*

Description: Not Tonight Deer is a powder which is mixed with water to spray on plants. When deer smell sprayed plants they are repelled by the smell of the eggs and deterred by the pepper. There are no sticking agents in the formulation so that Not Tonight Deer can be used on food crops. Therefore it will wash off in rain. Add a few teaspoons of cooking oil or a "spread sticker" (which you can buy at most nurseries) to increase the "stickability" of the product.

Product Name: Deerbusters Deer Repellent

Type: Taste & Odor

Product Formulation: Conc. and Powder

Active Ingredient(s): Putrescent eggs, garlic and capsaicin

Manufacturer: Deerbusters, 9735A Bethel Road, Frederick, MD 21702 Phone: 888-422-3337

Website: *www.deerbusters.com*

Description: DeerBusters Deer Repellent offers two methods of protection using both odor and taste. The repellent lasts for 3 months between applications under normal weather conditions, including rain. DeerBusters Deer Repellent includes three main ingredients: egg for longevity, garlic for odor, and pepper, for taste.

Product Name: Deerbusters Deer Repellent Sachets

Type: Odor

Product Formulation: RTU

Active Ingredient(s): Animal meal and red hot pepper

Manufacturer: Deerbusters 9735A Bethel Road, Frederick, MD 21702 Phone: 888-422-3337

Website: *www.deerbusters.com*

Description: In a convenient carrying pail, Deerbusters Deer Repellent Sachets are designed for specific plant protection. Hang them every few feet around flowers, trees, shrubs and vegetable gardens. Sachets are also used to control rabbits and raccoons. If sachets are being used in a vegetable garden they should be suspended from a stake at approximately a 3 ft height to keep them off of the vegetables and at the optimal deer browsing height.

Product Name: Deer Scram Deer & Rabbit Repellent

Type: Odor

Product Formulation: RTU

Active Ingredient(s): Dried blood, garlic, cloves, white pepper, and meat meal

Manufacturer: Enviro Protection Industries Co., 27 Link Drive, Suite C, Binghamton, NY 13904 Phone: 877-337-2726

Website: *www.deerscram.com*

Description: Deer Scram is all-natural, biodegradable and environmentally safe. Deer Scram won't harm animals, the environment or people. The scent of Deer Scram is not offensive to humans, though deer and rabbits will find it repulsive. Deer Scram can be applied year-round as a protective perimeter strip or it can be evenly spread over a garden bed or flowerbed. Apply consistently every 30-45 days.

Product Name: TerraCycle Deer Repellent

Type: Odor

Product Formulation: RTU

Active Ingredient(s): Putrescent eggs, peppermint oil and cinnamon

Manufacturer: TerraCycle Inc., 121 New York Avenue, Trenton, NJ 08638 Phone: 609-393-4252

Website: *www.terracycle.net*

Description: TerraCycle Deer Repellent is made from all-natural ingredients and packaged in recyled 1 liter soda bottles. Ready to use and made from all-natural ingredients, it also comes with a sprayer that fits on the bottles.

Product Name: Green Screen Deer Repellent

Type: Odor

Product Formulation: Bags Powder & RTU

Active Ingredient(s): Meat meal, red chili pepper

Manufacturer: Green Screen P.O. Box 451, Manistee, MI 49660
Phone: 800-968-9453

Website: *www.greenscreen1.com*

Description: Green Screen Deer Repellent Bags were developed in 1981 by a fruit grower in Michigan to protect her orchards from deer browsing damage. Green Screen is non-toxic, safe on edible crops, and stays effective after rainfall. Green Screen bags are hung approximately 2 feet apart, and 1 foot above the ground, to discourage deer and rabbits from browsing. Bags stay effective from three to six months.

Product Name: Fear Shake Away Deer & Large Animal Repellent

Type: Predator

Product Formulation: RTU

Active Ingredient(s): Bobcat, fox or coyote urine

Manufacturer: Bird-X, 300 N Elizabeth 2N, Chicago, IL 60607
Phone: 800-860-0473

Website: *www.bird-x.com*

Description: Shake Away is 100% organic, natural & safe! Shake Away is an effective all-natural animal repellent in a granular form. The distinctive ingredient is predator urine from coyote, fox or bobcat. One application lasts 90 days.

Product Name: Scoot Deer

Type: Taste

Product Formulation: RTU

Active Ingredient(s): Capsaicin and fatty acids

Manufacturer: Scoot Products, P.O. Box 150501, Grand Rapids, MI 49515 Phone: 800-460-7378

Website: *www.scootproducts.com*

Description: Scoot Deer contains food grade capsaicin that is used to repel deer for up to 30 days and is water resistant. It is a highly effective taste aversion repellent. What makes Scoot Deer unique is the addition of castor oil so, instead of having to reapply frequently, there is protection up to four weeks.

Product Name: Plant Saver All Natural Deer Repellent

Type: Odor

Product Formulation: RTU

Active Ingredient(s): Bone and meat meal, cloves and soap

Manufacturer: Cedar Creek 4010 Pope Road, Arbor Vitae, WI 54568 Phone: 715-385-9156

Website: *www.cedarcreekproducts.com*

Description: Plant Saver All Natural Deer Repellent is a natural formula that is safe to use on all shrubs and flowers. Fill each small inner bag with Plant Saver — tie bags shut and hang them every 2-3 feet in the garden or tie them on the branches of your fruit trees. Ten bags cover 40-50 linear feet and continue to work for up to 6 months.

Product Name: Deervik

Type: Odor

Product Formulation: RTU

Active Ingredient(s): Natural petroleum and fish by-products

Manufacturer: Deervik, P.O. Box 472, Sawyer, MI 49125
Phone: 269-426-6564

Website: *http://deervik.com*

Description: Deervik is a paste-like substance, not a spray. Place it on or near your plants, it is even safe to use with edible plants. There is no need to apply Deervik directly on plants. A small amount near the plant will do the job. It helps protect trees against damage in the fall when the bucks rub their antlers on trees and destroy bark too.

Product Name: Liquid Fence Deer & Rabbit Repellent

Type: Taste & Odor

Product Formulation: RTU & Conc.

Active Ingredient(s): Garlic and whole egg

Manufacturer: Liquid Fence Co., Inc. P.O. Box 300, Brodheadsville, PA 18322 Phone: 800-923-3623

Website: *www.liquidfence.com/deer-repellent.html*

Description: Liquid Fence is an all-natural deer repellent that is designed to offer year-round protection from deer and rabbits. It safely repels deer that are constantly foraging for food, eating evergreens, shrubs and other landscape plants.

Product Name: Deer Away

Type: Taste & Odor

Product Formulation: RTU & Conc.

Active Ingredient(s): Putrescent eggs

Manufacturer: Woodstream Corporation, 69 North Locust Street, Lititz, PA 17543 Phone: 717-626-2125

Website: *www.havahart.com*

Description: Deer Away prevents deer and rabbits from eating all types of plants. Apply it when deer and rabbits beginning to browse. Reapply every three months or more frequently if deer pressure is intense.

Certified Organic: Yes

Product Name: Deer Away Big Game Repellent

Type: Odor and Predator Fear

Product Formulation: Powder & Conc.

Active Ingredient(s): Capsaicin extracts, mustard oil, vegetable oil, lemon extract and putrescent eggs

Manufacturer: IntAgra, Inc. 8906 Wentworth Avenue South, Minneapolis, MN 55420 Phone: 800-800-1819

Website: *www.havahart.com*

Description: Deer Away Big-Game Repellent repels deer and rabbits from gardens, lawns, trees and shrubs. It repels animals with a deterrent odor that lasts 3 months. Will not harm trees.

Certified Organic: Yes

Product Name: Miller Hot Sauce Animal Repellent

Type: Taste

Product Formulation: Conc.

Active Ingredient(s): Capsaicin

Manufacturer: Miller Chemical & Fertilizer Co, P.O. Box 333, 120 Radio Road, Hanover, PA 17331 Phone: 717-632-8921

Website: *www.millerchemical.com*

Description: This browsing animal deterrent is derived from a cayenne pepper extract and is very effective against deer, rabbits, meadow and pine mice. Miller Hot Sauce Animal Repellent is effective on fruits, nut trees, vegetables, vine crops and ornamentals. Apply as a foliar spray to crops. Do not apply to the edible portions of food crops, unless you like really hot food!

Product Name: Deer Pharm

Type: Taste & Odor

Product Formulation: RTU & Conc.

Active Ingredient(s): Organic fish oils, vegetable juice, L-ascorbic acid, citric acid and soybean oil

Manufacturer: Pharm Solutions Inc., 2023 East Sims Way, Suite 358, Port Townsend, WA 98368 Phone: 805-927-7400

Website: *http://pharmsolutionsinc.com*

Description: Deer Pharm Deer Repellent is made with certified organic oils that repel deer with scent and taste. Spray it directly on shrubs, trees or plants in the evening. The aroma will dissipate overnight so people can't smell it the next day but deer can. Reapply frequently in the early season and less frequently as the season progresses.

Product Name: Plotsaver Liquid Deer Repellent

Type: Odor

Product Formulation: Conc.

Active Ingredient(s): Putrescent eggs, rosemary oil, mint oil, and vinegar

Manufacturer: Messina Wildlife Management, 55 Willow Street, Suite 1, Washington, NJ 07882 Phone: 908-320-7009

Website: *www.messinawildlife.com*

Description: Plotsaver Liquid Deer Repellent creates a powerful physical and sensory barrier that elk, moose, blacktail, mule, whitetail and other deer will not cross. Apply once every 30 days, regardless of weather. Will not wash off after heavy rain.

Certified Organic: Yes

Product Name: Deer Stopper

Type: Taste & Odor

Product Formulation: RTU

Active Ingredient(s): Putrescent eggs, vinegar, mint oil and rosemary oil

Manufacturer: Messina Wildlife Management, 55 Willow Street, Suite 1, Washington, NJ 07882 Phone: 908-320-7009

Website: *www.messinawildlife.com*

Description: Deer Stopper is a repellent composed of eggs, vinegar and other ingredients. It deters deer by both smell and taste and will dry clear and odor-free on all plants. This repellent can be applied to all shrubs, flowers, edible crops, forest, and fruit trees.

Product Name: Nature's Defense All Purpose Animal Repellent

Type: Odor

Product Formulation: RTU

Active Ingredient(s): Garlic, cinnamon, clove, white pepper, thyme, rosemary, and peppermint

Manufacturer: Nature's Defense P.O. Box 186, Zelienople, PA 16063 Phone: 866-947-9898

Website: *www.natures-defense.com*

Description: Animal control problems are easy, simply sprinkle Nature's Defense All Purpose Animal Repellents' organic formula around areas you want to protect. Animal problems will be solved quickly and easily. Apply Nature's Defense twice a week for the first two weeks, then once a week for maintenance. Lightly sprinkle granules in and around areas where animals are causing damage and or in areas you want to protect. Allow one week for Nature's Defense All Purpose Animal Repellent to take full effect.

Product Name: Nature's Defense Deer Repellent

Type: Odor

Product Formulation: RTU

Active Ingredient(s): Garlic and cinnamon

Manufacturer: Nature's Defense, P.O. Box 186, Zielenople, PA 16063
Phone: 866-947-9898

Website: *www.natures-defense.com*

Description: Nature's Defense Deer Repellent Packs are an effective and long lasting 60 day deer repellent. This weather-proof organic deer repellent is 100% safe and easy to use. Protect your valuable landscape and also feel confident when using it around children and pets.

Product Name: Deer Ban Deer Repellent

Type: Taste & Odor

Product Formulation: Conc.

Active Ingredient(s): 21 natural ingredients

Manufacturer: Deer Ban, 4204 Sunny Creek Lane, Apex, NC 27502
Phone: 800-371-0207

Website: *www.deerban.com*

Description: Deer Ban is an all-natural, powerful deer repellent that keeps deer away for 3-6 months per application and is simple to use. Deer Ban is weather-proof and does not smell bad. Deer Ban does not contain rotten eggs, urine or blood.

Product Name: BioDefend Deer Repellent

Type: Taste & Odor

Product Formulation: RTU & Conc

Active Ingredient(s): Putrescent eggs, white pepper and vinegar

Manufacturer: BioDefend, 150 Industrial Road, Alabaster, AL 35007
Phone: 800-653-3334

Website: *www.bio-defend.com*

Description: Keep deer and rabbits out of your garden with natural BioDefend Deer and Rabbit Repellent. BioDefend's deer repellent uses offensive smells and tastes to deer-proof plants without harming these common garden pests. It is environmentally friendly, children and pet safe.

Item	Product (Formulation)	Size	Approx. Cost
1.	BioDefend Deer Repellent (RTU)	16/32 oz.	$15-29
2.	BioDefend Deer Repellent (Conc.)	16/32 oz, 1/5 gal	$29-535
3.	Bobbex Deer Repellent (RTU)	32/48 oz.	$20-29
4.	Bobbex Deer Repellent (Conc.)	32 oz, 0.5/2.5/5 gal	$35-290
5.	Chase Deer Repellent Spray (RTU)	32 oz	$15
6.	Deer Away (RTU)	16/32 oz, 1 gal	$10-34
7.	Deer Away (Conc.)	16 oz/32 oz, 1 gal	$21-105
8.	Deer Away-Big Game Repellent (Conc.)	1 gal, 5 gal.	$21-85
9.	Deer Ban Deer Repellent (Conc.)	0.5 –10 gal.	$60-650
10.	Deer No No	8-96 packets	$40-290
11.	Deer Off (RTU)	16/32 oz	$10-18
12.	Deer Off (Conc.)	16/32 oz, 1/2.5 gal	$24-270
13.	Deer Pharm (RTU)	16 oz	$13
14.	Deer Pharm (Conc.)	1 gal	$95
15.	Deer Scram Deer & Rabbit Repellent (RTU)	2.5/6/25 lb	$19-118
16.	Deer Stopper (RTU)	32 oz, 1 gal	$15-32
17.	Deer Stopper (Conc.)	16/32 oz, 1 gal	$35-160
18.	Deerbusters Coyote Urine (RTU)	1 gal	$100
19.	Deerbusters Deer Repellent (Conc.)	2.5 gal	$290
20.	Deerbusters Deer Repellent Sachets (RTU)	16 oz.	$20
21.	Deervik (RTU)	1/7 lb	$20-75
22.	Dial Bar Soap (RTU)	4.5 oz	$1
23.	Green Screen Deer Repellent Bags (RTU)	20-200 packets	$20-160
24.	Hinder Deer & Rabbit Repellent (Conc.)	16 oz, 1 gal	$20-40
25.	Hot Pepper Wax Animal Repellent (RTU)	16 oz, 32 oz	$12-20
26.	Hot Pepper Wax Animal Repellent (Conc.)	1 gal	$40

Item	Product (Formulation)	Size	Approx. Cost
27.	Liquid Fence Deer & Rabbit Repellent (RTU)	32 oz, 1 gal	$13-25
28.	Liquid Fence Deer & Rabbit Repellent (Conc.)	40 oz, 1/2.5 gal	$40-260
29.	Miller Hot Sauce Animal Repellent (Conc.)	0.5 gal	$145
30.	Nature's Defense All Purpose Animal Repellent (RTU)	20 oz, 50 lb	$15-230
31.	Nature's Defense Deer Repellent (RTU)	15-150 packets	$50-400
32.	Not Tonight Deer! Repellent (RTU)	6 oz, 5 lb.	$13-70
33.	Plant Pro-Tec Deer & Rabbit Garlic Units (RTU)	25-250 clips	$20-130
34.	Plant Saver All Natural Deer Repellent (RTU)	2 lb	$30
35.	Plantskydd Animal Repellent (RTU)	1/3/7/20 lb	$10-90
36.	Plotsaver Liquid Deer Repellent (Conc.)	16/32 oz, 1 gal	$30-160
37.	Repellex Deer & Rabbit Repellent (RTU)	32 oz, 1 gal	$15-30
38.	Repellex Deer & Rabbit Repellent (Conc.)	32 oz, 1/2.5/5 gal	$35-475
39.	Scoot Deer (RTU)	32 oz	$19
40.	Scoot Deer (Conc.)	1 gal	$49
41.	Shake Away Deer & Large Animal Repellent (RTU)	20 oz, 3/12 lb	$15-100
42.	ShotGun Deer & Rabbit Repellent (RTU)	32 oz, 1 gal	$14-28
43.	ShotGun Hot Pepper Wax Animal Repellent (RTU)	32 oz.	$15
44.	ShotGun Repels-All (RTU)	1.25/3/6 lb	$12-29
45.	TerraCycle Deer Repellent (RTU)	1 litre	$15

EQUIPMENT

Item	Product (Formulation)	Size	Approx. Cost
46.	Wireless Deer Fence	3 posts	$60/5-25 ft
47.	Deer-X Deer Fence		$0.3/ft
48.	Deer Fence		$2-5/ft
49.	Scarecrow: Deer and Animal Repellent		$70
50.	Ultrasonic Motion Activated Deer & Animal Repeller		$65
51.	Deer Chaser Electronic Repeller		$59

Item	Product (Formulation)	Size	Approx. Cost
52.	Sonic: Deer and Animal Repeller		$99
53.	Spray Away Animal Repellant		$75
54.	Shishi odoshi – Deer Scarer		$30-45
55.	Bird Netting		$1-5/ft
56.	Floating Row Cover		$0.5/ft

INFORMATION RESOURCES
(State; Name; Website; Document Name)

Alabama; Alabama Cooperative Extension System; http://www.aces.edu/pubs/docs/A/ANR-0521/; *White-tailed Deer Management*

Alaska; University of Alaska Cooperative Extension Service; http://www.uaf.edu/ces/newsletters/mastergardeners/MGU04/MGU06_04.pdf; *Developing Browse Resistant Landscape Vegetation using Trees and Shrubs PDF*

Arkansas; University of Arkansas Division of Agriculture, Cooperative Extension Service; http://www.arhomeandgarden.org/landscaping/deer_resistant.htm; *Deer Resistant Plants*

Arizona; University of Arizona, College of Agriculture and Life Sciences; http://ag.arizona.edu/pubs/garden/az1237.pdf; *Deer and Rabbit Resistant Plants PDF*

California; University of California, Agriculture and Natural Resources; http://www.ipm.ucdavis.edu/PMG/PESTNOTES/pn74117.html; *Pests in Gardens and Landscapes-Deer*

Colorado; Colorado State University Extension; http://www.ext.colostate.edu/pubs/natres/06520.html; *Preventing Deer Damage*

Connecticut; University of Connecticut; http://www.hort.uconn.edu/IPM/general/htms/deer.htm; *Animal Damage Control-White Tailed Deer*

Florida; University of Florida IFSA Extension; http://edis.ifas.ufl.edu/uw128; *Coping with Deer Damage in Florida PDF*

Georgia; University of Georgia Cooperative Extension; http://pubs.caes.uga.edu/caespubs/horticulture/deer.html; *Deer Tolerant Ornamental Plants PDF*

Georgia; Georgia Department of Natural Resources-Wildlife Resources Division; http://georgiawildlife.dnr.state.ga.us/content/displaycontent. asp?txtDocument=123&txtPage=2; *Controlling Deer Damage in Georgia*

Hawaii; Hawai'i Conservation Alliance; http://hawaiiconservation.org/_library/documents/ungulates_2007_web.pdf; *Controlling Wild Sheep and Deer on Conservation Land in Hawai'I PDF*

Idaho; University of Idaho Cooperative Extension Service; http://www.cnr.uidaho.edu/extforest/WL8.pdf; *Control Deer and Elk Browse Damage PDF*

Illinois; University of Illinois Extension; http://web.extension.uiuc.edu/champaign/homeowners/981205.html; *Reducing Deer Damage to Landscape Plants*

Indiana; Perdue University Extension Service; http://www.ces.purdue.edu/ces/Vanderburgh/horticulture/extnotes/2005/deer.htm; *Deer Damage Detrimental*

Iowa; City of Iowa City, Iowa; http://www.icgov.org/default/?id=1607; *Deer Resistant Landscaping PDF*

Kansas; Kansas State University Agricultural Experiment Station and Cooperative Extension Service; http://www.oznet.ksu.edu/library/wldlf2/C728.PDF; *Deer Damage Control Options PDF*

Kentucky; University of Kentucky, College of Agriculture Co-operative Extension; http://www.ca.uky.edu/agc/pubs/for/for57/for57.htm; *Managing White-tailed Deer in Kentucky*

Louisiana; Louisiana State University AgCenter; http://www.lsuagcenter.com/en/lawn_garden/home_gardening/landscaping/Deer+in+the+Landscape.htm; *Deer in the Landscape*

Maine; University of Maine Cooperative Extension; http://www.umext.maine.edu/piscataquis/gardening/2007/Vol5Iss6/deer.htm; *Deer in My Garden!*

Maryland; Maryland Department of Natural Resources; http://www.dnr.state.md.us/wildlife/ddmtintro.asp; *Maryland Deer Damage Management Techniques*

Massachusetts; University of Massachusetts Amherst Extension; http://www.umassvegetable.org/soil_crop_pest_mgt/articles_html/preventing_deer_damage.html; *Preventing Deer Damage*

Michigan; Michigan State University Extension; http://web1.msue.msu.edu/imp/modwl/11209805.html; *Fencing for Deer Damage Control*

Minnesota; University of Minnesota Extension Services; http://www.extension.umn.edu/projects/yardandgarden/ygbriefs/h462deer-coping.html; *Coping With Deer in Home Landscapes*

Mississipi; Mississippi Department of Wildlife, Fisheries and Parks; http://www.mdwfp.com/Level2/Wildlife/Game/Deer/Articles.asp?Keywords =Management; *Mississippi Wildlife Fisheries and Parks Deer Program Management Articles*

Missouri; University of Missouri Extension; http://extension.missouri.edu/explore/miscpubs/mp0685.htm; *Controlling Deer Damage in Missouri PDF*

Montana; Montana State University Extension Service; http://www.montana.edu/wwwpb/pubs/mt9814.html; *Minimizing Deer Damage to Residential Plantings*

Nebraska; University of Nebraska-Lincoln; http://www.ianrpubs.unl.edu/epublic/pages/publicationD.jsp?publicationId=931; *Managing Deer Damage in Nebraska*

Nebraska; University of Nebraska-Lincoln, Institute of Agriculture and Natural Resources, Cooperative Extension Division; http://icwdm.org/handbook/mammals/mam_d25.pdf; *Prevention and Control of Wildlife Damage- Deer PDF*

Nevada; Nevada Department of Wildlife; http://ndow.org/wild/animals/facts/mule_deer.shtm; *Nevada Wildlife-Mule Deer*

New Hampshire; University of New Hampshire Cooperative Extension; http://extension.unh.edu/Pubs/AgPubs/Apft5214.pdf; *Controlling Deer Damage in New England Orchards PDF*

New Jersey; Rutgers, The State University of New Jersey, NJ Cooperative Extension; http://www.montana.edu/wwwpb/pubs/mt9521.html; *Landscape Plants Rated for Deer Resistance PDF*

New Mexico; New Mexico Game and Fish; http://www.wildlife.state.nm.us/publications/documents/urbandeer.pdf; *Mule Deer in Urban Neighborhoods PDF*

New York; Cornell University Cooperative Extension Forestry; http://www.dnr.cornell.edu/ext/bmp/contents/nonharvest/non_damage.htm; *Preventing Deer Damage to Young Trees PDF*

New York; Cornell University Department of Natural Resources Cooperative Extension; http://www.dnr.cornell.edu/ext/chdp/Reducingdeerdamage. htm; *Reducing Deer Damage Home to Gardens and Landscape Plantings PDF*

North Carolina; Duke Forest Management; http://www.env.duke.edu/forest/ forest/deer_broch.pdf; *Reducing Deer Damage on your Property PDF*

North Dakota; North Dakota State University Cooperative Extension; http:// www.ext.nodak.edu/extnews/hortiscope/pests/deer.htm; *Questions on Deer*

Ohio; Ohio State University Extension; http://guernsey.osu.edu/master-gar- deners/drought-deer-resistant-plants; *Drought and Deer Resistant Plants*

Oklahoma; Oklahoma Cooperative Extension; http://pods.dasnr.okstate.edu/ docushare/dsweb/Get/Document-2700/NREM-9009web%20color.pdf; *Ecology and Management of Deer in Oklahoma PDF*

Oklahoma; Oklahoma State University Cooperative Extension; http://osuex- tra.okstate.edu/pdfs/F-6427web.pdf; *Ornamental and Garden Plants: Controlling Deer Damage PDF*

Oregon; Oregon State University Extension; http://extension.oregonstate.edu/ catalog/pdf/ec/ec1557.pdf; *Reducing Deer Damage in Your Yard PDF*

Pennsylvania; Penn State Cooperative Extension Pike County; http://pike.exten- sion.psu.edu/Horticulture/DeerResistantPlants.pdf; *Deer Resistant Plants*

Rode Island; University of Rode Island; http://www.uri.edu/research/sust- land/deerlist.html; *Plants Least Preferred by Deer*

South Carolina; Clemson University Cooperative Extension service; http:// virtual.clemson.edu/groups/psapublishing/PAGES/AFW/AFW6.pdf; *Reducing Deer Damage at Home and on the Farm PDF*

South Dakota; South Dakota State University Extension Service; http://hort- mg.sdstate.edu/Oct%2024_2005.doc; *Deer-proof Plants*

Tennessee; University of Tennessee Agriculture Extension Service; http:// www.utextension.utk.edu/publications/spfiles/SP598.pdf; *Single-strand Fencing to Manage Deer Damage*

Texas; The Texas A & M University System; http://plantanswers.tamu.edu/ publications/deerbest.html; *Deer in the Urban Landscape*

Utah; Utah Division of Wildlife Management; http://wildlife.utah.gov/hunting/ biggame/pdf/mule_deer_plan.pdf; *Mule Deer Management Program PDF*

Vermont; University of Vermont Extension Services; http://www.uvm.edu/~pass/perry/oh64.html; *Deer Resistant Perennials*

Virginia; Virginia Cooperative Extension; http://www.ext.vt.edu/news/periodicals/commhort/1997-10/1997-10-02.html; *Low Cost Slant Fence Excludes Deer from Plantings PDF*

Washington; Washington State University Spokane County Extension; http://www.spokane-county.wsu.edu/Spokane/eastside/Fact%20Sheets/C063%20Deer%20Resistant%20Plants.pdf; *Deer Resistant Plants*

West Virginia; West Virginia Division of Natural Resources; http://www.wvdnr.gov/Hunting/IntAppDeerCon.shtm; *An Integrated Approach to Deer Damage Control*

Wisconsin; University of Wisconsin Extension; http://learningstore.uwex.edu/pdf/G3083.pdf; *Controlling Deer Damage in Wisconsin PDF*

Wyoming; Wyoming Animal Damage Management Board; http://www.wyadmb.com/index.htm;

GENERAL

The Internet Center for Wildlife Damage Management;
http://209.85.215.104/search?q=cache:Xiipz_ksbyoJ:attra.ncat.org/attra-pub/deercontrol.html+alabama+deer+resistant+plants&hl=en&ct=clnk&cd=14&gl=us;

Appropriate Technology Transfer for Rural Areas (ATTRA); http://www.attra.ncat.org/attra-pub/PDF/deercontrol.pdf; Deer Control Options

State Extension; http://www.extension.org/pages/Deer; Deer

DEER-PROOF BOOKS

Creating a Deer Proof Garden by Peter Derano, 2007, Self Published

Wildlife in the Garden: How to Live in Harmony with Deer, Raccoons, Rabbits, Crows, and Other Pesky Creatures by Gene Logsdon, 1999, Indiana University Press

Deerproofing Your Yard & Garden by Rhonda Massingham Hart, 2005, Storey Publishing

Gardening in Deer Country (Gardening Guides Series) by Vincent Drzewucki, 1998, Brick Tower Publishing

Flowerbeds & Borders in Deer Country by Vincent Drzewucki, 2003, Brick Tower Books

Deer of the Southwest: A Complete Guide to the Natural History, Biology, and Management of Southwestern Mule Deer and White-tailed Deer by Jim Heffelfinger, 2006, Texas A&M Press

Outwitting Deer: 101 Truly Ingenious Methods and Proven Techniques to Prevent Deer from Devouring your Garden and Destroying Your Yard by Bill Adler Jr., 1999, The Lyons Press

Solving Deer Problems: How to Keep them Out of your Garden, Avoid them on the Road, and Deal with Them Anywhere! by Peter Loewer, 2002, The Lyons Press

Deer in my Garden Volume 1 Perennials & Subshrubs by Carolyn Singer, 2006, Garden Wisdom Press

Deer in my Garden Volume 2 Groundcovers & Edgers by Carolyn Singer, 2008, Garden Wisdom Press

Gardening Among Deer without Hiring a Mountain Lion: Invite Deer into your Beautiful Garden Every Day by Yvonne Baron Estes, 2005, Ponyfoot Press

14

Mission Accomplished

Ten years have passed since I finished writing "Preventing Deer Damage." Now as a result, thousands of gardeners are better prepared to survive in deer country with some semblance of success.

Initially on my own property, we had secured about four acres of gardens and orchards and left the rest of the forest for the deer and the multitudes of animals such as bear, elk and various carnivores that roamed our remote mountaintop retreat. Our land had escaped the ravages of nearby forest fires, our view of the Columbia River was still pristine with no other habitation in sight and our old lumber trail road was as hazardous as ever. It seems an 18% grade always maintains its steepness and never ceases to make the heart pound a bit when coming up in the middle of winter with a tire-chained ATV pulling a dogsled full of supplies.

Life was good. The 30 trees in the orchard were now too prolific. We had cut the cultivation of our 100 ft x 50 ft vegetable garden in half, had laid in over 30 cords of fir and larch firewood and Elaine had finally finished most of her projects.

In between times, we had managed to travel to almost 100 foreign countries. Some of these travels were with backpacks that lasted 5 or 6 months and occurred during the winter to places like Western China and Tibet, every part of Indonesia from Borneo through Irian Jaya to the Komodo Islands and finally to Antarctica on a Russian research ship.

But trouble was brewing. The deer had lost the war, the gardens were expansive and mature and we had enough firewood for the next ten years. We were getting restless and it was time for a change. So, we decided to sell the house, buy a small RV and travel the U.S.A. for a few years. Our health was good, although I could see my 80th birthday just a few years ahead. Thankfully, Elaine's Northern Minnesota homesteading family genes kept her energy level and physical strength equal to that of an athlete in training.

The house sold quickly, we found a low mileage, previously owned Roadtrek 20' camper and we were on our way. With our books and travel mementos stored away, furniture and vehicles disposed of — we were free as birds. Elaine had been studying the U.S. Presidents in the order of their time in office, as well as other important people of the time such as the Presidential wives, Franklin, Burr, Hamilton and MacArthur. This helped in our somewhat loose and erratic planning, as we wanted to see as many of the historical sites and museums as possible. We drove 46,000 miles during the next 18 months and saw most of the United States, many of which we had been in before but now our destinations were more specific. We took a break from the camper by taking a trip to Tasmania, Western Australia and Singapore. Being in Singapore for Chinese New Year was something special.

We have now settled in a civilized home in Spokane, Washington. It has taken a few adjustments, but that's what the progression through life is all about. A new way of life, new friends and new adventures! Traveling is still on the horizon, with another road trip planned through parts of the Midwest and south that we missed. This time instead of a camper, we are returning to our roots and will camp in the small tent we had used for many years while exploring the canoeing waters of Ontario's Quetico Provincial Park and Minnesota. Our passports are up-to-date and Spain and Portugal are on the list for next year.

Sometimes there are unexpected happenings that make a story complete. When we notified our customers that we were no longer able to continue to distribute "Preventing Deer Damage" due to our planned travels, one of our first customers and old friends, Acres U.S.A. offered to continue the printing and distribution of the book, and was also interested in updating it and improving the overall format. What you have now is a very professional edition of a small pamphlet that had just evolved from some personal observations. I am deeply indebted to the entire staff, particularly researcher/editor Anne Van Nest and artist Bryan Kight at Acres U.S.A. for their interest and hard work to keep the publication alive and well.

Robert G. Juhre
August 2008

Index